Short Bike Rides™

in and around Chicago

D0043202

Help Us Keep
This Guide Up to Date

Every effort has been made by the author and editors to make this guide as accurate and useful as possible. However, many things can change after a guide is published—establishments close, phone numbers change, facilities come under new management, and so on.

We would love to hear from you concerning your experiences with this guide and how you feel it could be made better and be kept up to date. While we may not be able to respond to all comments and suggestions, we'll take them to heart, and we'll also make certain to share them with the author. Please send your comments and suggestions to the following address:

The Globe Pequot Press
Reader Response/Editorial
Department
P.O. Box 833
Old Saybrook, CT 06475

Or you may e-mail us at:

editorial@globe-pequot.com

Thanks for your input, and happy travels!

Short Bike Rides™

in and around Chicago

BY
CHRISTOPHER PERCY COLLIER

The Globe Pequot Press

Old Saybrook, Connecticut

Cover design: Saralyn D'Amato-Twomey
Cover photograph: West Stock
Text design: Lisa Reneson
Map design: Erin Hernandez
Interior photos provided by: Christopher P. Collier

Library of Congress Cataloging-in-Publication Data

Collier, Christopher P.
    Short bike rides in and around Chicago / by Christopher P.
Collier. — 1st Ed.
        p.   cm.   — (Short bike rides series)
        ISBN 0-7627-0410-1
        1. Cycling—Illinois—Chicago Metropolitan Area—Guide-
books. 2. Chicago Metropolitan Area (Ill.)—Guidebooks. I. Title.
II. Series.
GV1045.5.I32C455   1999
917.73'110433—dc21   99–18235
                                                                CIP

Contents

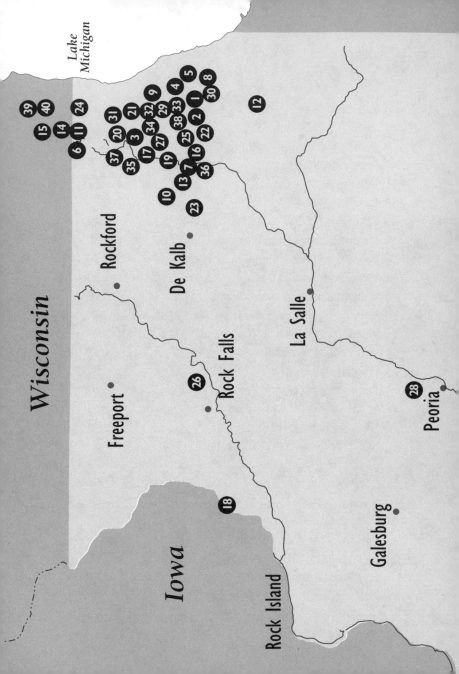

Introduction

Open up a can of Chicagoland bike rides. Let 'em spill out on the table where you make your most crucial decisions. Get a map out. Okay, where's it gonna be? The first rails-to-trail conversion in the country? Mountain biking in Wisconsin? How about the Chicago Botanical Gardens? Maybe a city ride into the Historic Prairie District? Or down into the wonders of Hyde Park? Even better, how about a trek clear across the state for a ride along the Mississippi River?

All it takes is a plan and a push. Sometimes it's hard to get away. It's difficult to leave all that's going on at work and home. That's why this book is important: It makes getting to the outdoors as easy and enjoyable as possible, getting you out the door with a plan.

For us Chicagolanders, getting out is part of our identity. We thrive on staying active even when it gets cold and windy. Out-of-staters from other big cities marvel at how we do it. It's not something you can explain; it's something you have to live to know. The ice breaks and spring knocks. Chicago and its suburbs explode. People are outside in droves. City streets, sidewalk cafes, and city parks are packed. The forest preserves are overrun in our frenzied embrace of the outdoors.

We don't have mountains like on the West Coast. We don't have a handful of big cities we can get to in under three hours like the East Coast. We have the outdoors. We have what was named by early planners *Urbs in horto*—"a city set in a garden."

About the Rides

The term *short bike rides* may be a misnomer to some. It all depends on what you consider to be a long ride. These range from 5 to 30 miles, and often there are opportunities for you to shorten or lengthen them as you deem appropriate.

Almost all of these rides are geared for casual bikers. Still, mountain biking, which can be more physical, has become so popular with people of all ages that it would be a slight not to include some of these riveting trails!

These rides are mostly situated around Chicagoland—a term that loosely refers to places near Chicago. I broke the rules a little to give you some of the best rides around, however. Most are within two hours of downtown Chicago, and no ride is farther away than about three hours.

Directions take you as close to the trailhead as possible. I've chosen city parking places with safety and frugality in mind. The mile-by-mile directions will give you an idea where you are if you have an odometer on your bike. They'll also tell you what streets to turn on and what landmarks you'll pass so you'll know you're on the right course. Though they're not drawn to scale, the trail maps will orient you as to where you are and what's within reach. And each ride begins with a brief overview, giving you all of the information you need to choose a trail: attractions, terrain, distance, approximate pedaling time, food, and facilities.

Be Prepared

There are certain habits you get into when preparing for a bike ride. I've learned that bringing the right things is like an art form: You don't want to be weighed down, but you don't want too little. On many bikes, you can attach a small bag beneath the seat. In this pouch, keep the tools necessary to work on your bike while on the ride. Tinkering and tightening brakes, seats, wheels, and other parts of your bike often makes a world of difference when something is not right while on the trail. Tools for fixing broken chains and flat tires are also helpful once you learn how to use them. It's important to bring at least one warm layer, too. If clouds are in the sky, that layer should be rain resistant unless you want to get wet. Never underestimate the possibility of rain. In the car, keep something a little warmer for the drive home.

The following lists are things that I consider essential and helpful for riding my bike in Chicagoland.

Essential Tools	Recommended Tools
Air pump	Backpack or hip bag
Allen wrenches	Camera
Bike lock	Cellular phone
Helmet	Compass
Identification	Sunscreen
Money	**Clothing**
Safety whistle	Biking gloves
Spare inner tube	Hat
Tire irons	Sneakers
Trail map	Waterproof windbreaker
Tube patching kit	**Other Equipment**
Watch	Bike rack
Water bottle	Bungee cords
	Chain lubricant
	Headlight
	Odometer
	Road map

Safety

The rides that I have chosen for this guide are for the most part in safe areas, but crime and other dangers in and around the city is a fact of life. It's a good idea to bike with a friend and to carry a whistle just in case.

The neighborhoods that surround the following rides in this book may call for more heightened awareness: Uptown, Logan Square, Route 66 Starting Point, Lakefront South, and Hyde Park. Also, though there are leash laws in Chicago and in many of the forest preserves, some dog owners have a tendency to let their dogs run free. My advice is to be wary of strangers and free roaming dogs when biking on a remote trail.

Cities are often dangerous places, but with the right precautions, staying out of harm's way can be accomplished. Most everyone I know who rides a bike in the city wears a helmet, brings a bike lock that can lock two tires and a bike frame, and takes their bike seat with them when they lock up.

While it's not anywhere near as bad as other large cities, riding in Chicago when cars are present requires that you keep your hands on your brakes at all times. Be especially observant when riding along rows of parked cars. One of the most common urban biking accidents occurs when a parked car's door is suddenly opened unbeknownst to a cyclist riding by. Take it slow, enjoy the surroundings, and stay alert.

Children

Chicago tries its best to be a bike-friendly city. There are many places to lock your bike and designated bike lanes on more city streets than you'd expect. However, I strongly discourage bringing small children on city rides that have even moderate car or bike traffic. It is extremely difficult to watch traffic *and* young children, who may not understand the dangers of the road.

The following suburban rides, however, are family friendly: the southern section of Robert McClory Bike Path; Fox River Trails; Tinley Creek; Des Plaines Trail; Busse Woods; Chain O' Lakes State Park; Deer Grove; North Branch; Old Plank Road Trail; Waterfall Glen; Salt Creek; Great River Trail; I & M Canal State Trail; and the

Skokie Trail. These rides are far from city traffic and crowds of erratic, high-speed bikers. These rides are also more suitable for children as they tend to have rest rooms, water fountains, and some form of patrol nearby.

Reader Feedback

Rides and road conditions change over time. Feel free to contact me about any changes you find in the rides in this book. You can e-mail me at cpercycoll@aol.com or write me in care of The Globe Pequot Press, P.O. Box 833, Old Saybrook, CT 06475.

THE TIN MAN
from
The Wizard of Oz
by Frank Baum
Welcomes You
to
OZ PARK

A Heartfelt Salute
to the Community
from the
LINCOLN PARK
CHAMBER OF COMMERCE

October 1995

Belmont Antiques/Armitage Boutique

Number of miles:	7.5
Approximate pedaling time:	2½ hours
Terrain:	Flat
Traffic:	Heavy
Things to see:	Antiques shops, charming boutiques
Food and facilities:	Four Farthings, Beat Kitchen, and many other places along Armitage Avenue

With items old and new, this ride offers the best of both worlds for power shoppers and browsers. It takes you through the beautiful portion of Chicago known as Lincoln Park and to the heart of city antiquing.

Park on one of the charming Lakeview streets north and east of Ashland Avenue. Find your way onto Lincoln Avenue, one of only a few Chicago streets that angles southeast through the city. Sunlight shoots an orange hue down this wide corridor during late hours of the day. This part of Lincoln Avenue is slowly transforming for the better as more shops crop up. It's an extension of the main stem of antiques stores on Belmont Avenue that you'll pass toward the end of the ride.

South of Wrightwood Avenue is Lincoln Park central, which means scores of young people. Lincoln Park is known as the stomping grounds for a young and affluent twenty- and thirty-something crowd. As the city expands and property values continue to skyrocket, it's growing clear that Lincoln Park bars are frequented by younger professional crowds and Lincoln Park homes by older, more well-to-do professionals.

I

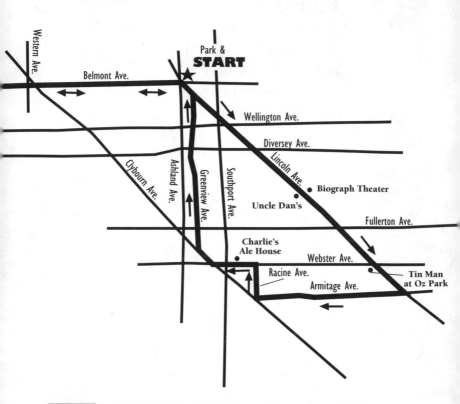

HOW TO GET THERE

From the northern suburbs, head southeast on I–94. Exit east onto Addison Avenue, then head south on Ashland Avenue to the three-way intersection of Belmont, Lincoln, and Ashland Avenues. Park on residential side streets east of Ashland, north or south of Belmont Avenue.

DIRECTIONS

FOR

THE RIDE

0.0 From Belmont Avenue, pedal south on Lincoln Avenue.

0.5 Lincoln Avenue intersects with Southport and Wellington Avenues.

1.4 Pass Uncle Dan's Outfitters on right. Biograph Theater is on left.

1.9 Pass Tin Man Sculpture on corner of Oz Park.

2.1 Pass Four Farthings Pub on left.

2.3 Turn right onto Armitage Avenue.

3.0 Pass Active Endeavors on left.

3.3 Turn right onto Racine Avenue.

3.5 Turn left onto Webster Avenue.

3.7 Pass Charlie's Ale House.

3.9 Turn right onto Clybourn Avenue.

4.6 Turn right onto Greenview Avenue.

5.3 Turn left onto Belmont Avenue.

6.0 Pass Beat Kitchen on right at 2100 West Belmont Avenue.

6.5 At Western Avenue, turn around on Belmont Avenue.

7.5 Cross Lincoln Avenue and return to your starting point.

Pass the famous Biograph Theater. Here a mannequin sits in an old booth along with a newspaper announcing the 1934 death of notorious bank robber John Dillinger, who had been proclaimed "Public Enemy #1" by then FBI director J. Edgar Hoover. He was ambushed by FBI agents on his way out of the theater.

Still on Lincoln, south of Fullerton Avenue you'll enter an area notorious for its bar scene. Renowned for its blue "Shark-bite" cocktails—served in a fish bowl with a handful of straws and a rubber shark to boot—Bamboo Bernie's is the most garish of the lot.

Once you reach Armitage Avenue, the chichi shops start, where you can find everything from dresses to hand-carved wooden boxes, exotic jewelry, and high-end outdoor gear. Though it's a tad more residential, Webster Avenue hosts a scattering of boutiques and restaurants.

At Belmont Avenue the scene changes. Things get more industrial as you pick your way through antiques shops located along what's called Antique Row. Each shop has its own specialty and charm. If you're looking for modern memorabilia, head to Twentieth Century Revue. If you're looking for antique watches, check out Father Time. If you're looking for antique radios, venture into Good Old Days. There are enough shops that you can work one side of the street on your way to Western Avenue and the other as you return.

Southport Ride

Number of miles:	7.2
Approximate pedaling time:	3 hours
Terrain:	Flat
Traffic:	Heavy
Things to see:	Prairie-style architecture, churches, the Music Box Theater, Alta Vista
Food and facilities:	Red Tomato, Cafe Zinc, China Lite, Hi Ricky, Cullens Tavern, Uncommon Ground, Viennese Hauss Brandt

Southport Avenue got its name in the 1840s, when stagecoaches drove down this wide Chicago thoroughfare bound for Milwaukee. Stage teamsters called Milwaukee "north port" and Chicago "south port." Chi-town natives will tell you that not more than a decade ago Southport was a no-man's-land, too far west to be considered a desirable neighborhood. Nowadays, cafe culture dominates this commercial street. A prime spot for good food and storefront gazing, its wide roadway and sidewalks accommodate constant foot traffic. Lined with attractive single-family and two-flat residences, neighboring residential streets are arched over with great green branches.

The steeple of the St. Alphonsus Parish, visible from many blocks away, helps give Southport its distinct identity. The ride begins 1 block south of the church at the site of Zum Deutschen Ek, a pretty good German pub and restaurant.

For the first half mile, notice that many storefront corners are crowned with small rounded towers, a style made popular by a

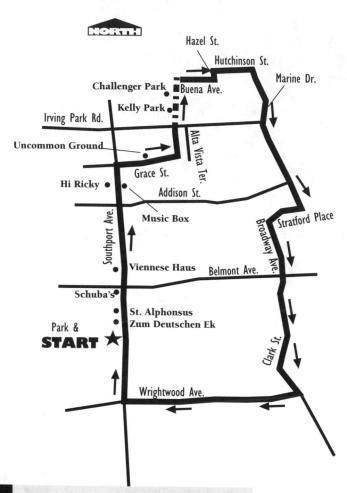

NORTH

Hazel St.

Hutchinson St.

Marine Dr.

Challenger Park

Buena Ave.

Kelly Park

Irving Park Rd.

Uncommon Ground

Alta Vista Ter.

Grace St.

Hi Ricky

Addison St.

Music Box

Stratford Place

Broadway Ave.

Southport Ave.

Viennese Haus

Belmont Ave.

Schuba's

St. Alphonsus
Zum Deutschen Ek

Clark St.

Park &
START

Wrightwood Ave.

HOW TO GET THERE

From I–94, exit east at Diversey Avenue.
Turn north onto Southport Avenue. Park
along the street in the vicinity of Oakdale
Avenue, south of Lincoln Avenue.

DIRECTIONS
FOR
THE RIDE

0.0 From Zum Deutschen Ek on Southport Avenue, head north.

0.1 Pass St. Alphonsus Parish.

0.3 Pass Schuba's Bar and Grill.

0.6 Pass under Southport Avenue brown line El stop. Pass Viennese Hauss Brandt coffee shop on right, next to Bistrot Zinc.

1.0 Pass Music Box movie theater and Cullens Tavern on right; Hi Ricky is on left.

1.1 Turn right onto Grace Street.

1.2 Pass Uncommon Ground coffee shop on left.

1.5 Turn left onto Seminary Avenue.

1.6 Turn right onto Byron Street.

1.7 Turn right onto Alta Vista turnaround.

1.8 Turn left onto Byron.

1.9 Enter Kelly Park.

2.2 Enter Challenger Park.

2.3 Pass under El tracks to take right onto Buena Avenue.

2.4 Pass church on left.

2.5 Turn left onto Hazel Street.

2.6 Turn right onto Hutchinson Street.

2.8 Turn right onto Marine Drive.

4.3 Turn right onto Strafford Place.

4.4 Turn left onto Broadway Avenue.

5.2 Broadway turns into Clark Street at intersection.

5.6 Turn right onto Wrightwood Avenue.

6.8 Turn right onto Southport Avenue.

7.2 Return to your car around Oakdale Avenue.

nineteenth-century architectural movement known as Richardsonian Romanesque. As you continue north you'll pass Schuba's, Belport Liquor, Southport Lanes, Starbucks, and Justin's, all bearing this motif.

After the Southport El stop, prepare for olfactory overload: A

cosmopolitan swirl of aromas emanates from local restaurants and runs the culinary gamut. Check out sticky buns from Ann Sather; Viennese pastries from Viennese Hauss Brandt (they also serve a coffee milk shake with real coffee grounds that's out of this world); chic French fare from Bistrot Zinc; dumplings from China Lite; fresh tortillas from Mamacitas; offbeat Continental cuisine from the Still Life Cafe, Dish, and Cullens; Thai food from Hi Ricky; and Italian fare from Strega Nona and Deleece.

Across from Hi Ricky is another Southport landmark, the Music Box Theater. Paul Gapp, a *Chicago Tribune* architectural critic, described the inside of the Music Box well when he wrote, "The architectural style is an eclectic mélange of Italian, Spanish and Pardon-My-Fantasy put together with passion" (*Arts and Books,* July 31, 1983). The Music Box was constructed in 1929, when sound had just been introduced to movies. As a result, space was left for an orchestra pit and organ chambers just in case audio didn't fly. Immersed in red curtains, baroque-style moldings, and a cloud-painted ceiling that turns to stars when the lights go out, artsy films roll on its silver screens.

Your next stop is the Alta Vista Terrace District, built between 1900 and 1904. Designated a Chicago landmark by the city council, this lovely strip of brownstone homes is the same on one side of the street as the other, minor variations aside. As you begin at one end, you can find—across the street and at the other end—a duplicate house. Once you hit the middle, the houses across from each other look identical.

A mile or so later you'll enter another North Side secret: Beautiful Prairie Style houses are tucked away along Hutchinson and Hazel in this unassuming locale. On your return south, you'll pass parks and favorable addresses just a hop, skip, and jump away from the lakefront.

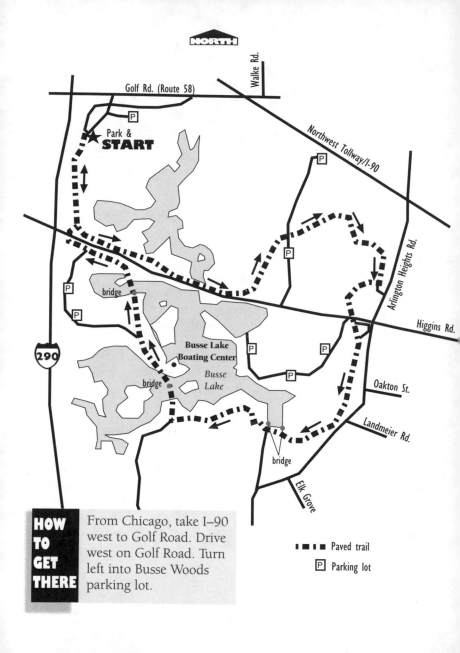

NORTH

Golf Rd. (Route 58)

Walke Rd.

Northwest Tollway/I-90

P

Park &
START

P

Arlington Heights Rd.

Higgins Rd.

290

bridge

P

P

**Busse Lake
Boating Center**

*Busse
Lake*

bridge

P

P

P

Oakton St.

Landmeier Rd.

bridge

Elk Grove

**HOW
TO
GET
THERE**

From Chicago, take I–90
west to Golf Road. Drive
west on Golf Road. Turn
left into Busse Woods
parking lot.

▪ ▪ ▪ Paved trail
P Parking lot

3 **Busse Woods**

Number of miles:	9.4
Approximate pedaling time:	3½ hours
Terrain:	Flat, well-maintained, paved
Traffic:	None
Things to see:	Busse Lake
Food and facilities:	Rest rooms and picnic tables near parking lot at start of ride

Busse Woods is one of eight bicycle trails in Chicago's Cook County and definitely one of the best. You'll be in and out of dark forests and open fields for most of the trail while patches of Busse Lake come and go. There are no hills—just winding pavement. It's the perfect preserve for those who want to coast along without a care in the world.

With its paved trails, boating center, and series of meadows, Busse Woods Reserve is about biking, skating, running, boating, fishing, and taking advantage of open space. Also known as the Ned Brown Preserve, this 3,700-acre holding is formed around the 590-acre expanse of Busse Lake.

You'll find access to the trail at the Northwestern Division Headquarters off Route 53 between Higgins Road and Golf Road. At 0.6 mile, right after the first bridge, you'll enter one of many brief stretches of forest. If it's a sunny day, each stand of mature woodland will make your eyes readjust to the forest shade. These short touches of forest are good opportunities to cool off.

The smooth trail surface at your ride's outset will make it easy to slowly gain momentum in your lower gears—but be on the

DIRECTIONS

FOR

THE RIDE

0.0 Turn left out of parking lot.

0.8 Turn left at fork parallel to Higgins Road.

1.6 Pass parking lot.

2.0 Pass another parking lot.

2.6 Pass third parking lot.

4.5 Cross overpass.

5.5 Pass parking lot.

6.0 Veer right.

6.9 Veer right.

7.5 Pass another parking lot.

8.6 Cross Higgins Road and veer left on trail.

9.4 Return to your car.

lookout for in-line skaters. Because Busse Woods is one of the few forest preserves paved well enough to skate on, dry days bring many skaters here.

At 1.8 miles and after passing the second parking area, you'll get your first up-close and personal glimpse at the northern section of Busse Lake. The larger portion of Busse Lake is south of Higgins Road. Short stretches of forest and meadow are only enough to tease you for these first few miles, but after you pass the third parking lot, you'll get a healthy 3-mile dose of wooded scenery.

There's less congestion in this eastern area of the preserve, making it easier to build a good steady pace. At the Higgins Road Overpass, switch to a higher gear and head up the short incline to avoid automotive traffic—or stay on the lower path to your right and walk your bike across.

At about 5.5 miles the trail veers back westward and you slowly begin to see less forest and more open prairie. As you cross two short bridges, you'll see the bulk of Busse Lake stretching in all directions.

At 7.1 miles you'll pass the Busse Lake Boating Center, where you can rent small sailboats and explore the preserve by water. While you're on the water, small armies of frogs will leap from lily pads as you approach, and ducks paddle about uninterrupted.

Tucked away from nearby suburban residences and interstate highways, this is a pleasant, insulated pedal. For a mellow low-maintenance ride, there's very little you can say about Busse Woods that's not complimentary.

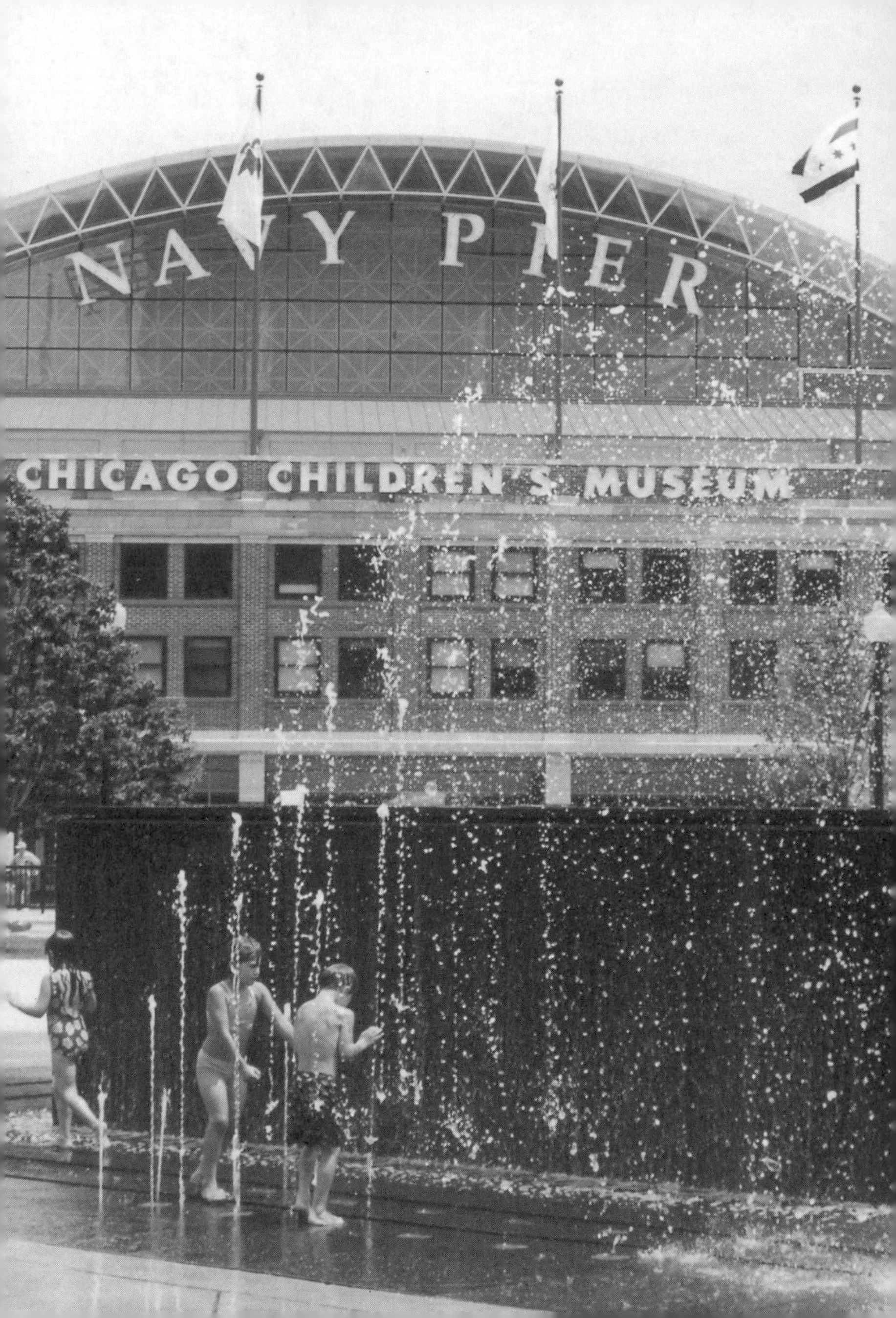
CHICAGO CHILDREN'S MUSEUM

4 Lakefront North

Number of miles:	17.4
Approximate pedaling time:	4½ hours
Terrain:	Flat, well maintained
Traffic:	None
Things to see:	Lake Michigan, Chess Pavilion, Navy Pier
Food and Facilities:	Waveland Cafe, Ranalli's Lakeside, Burritoville, Ed Debevics, Montrose Harbor, Theater on the Lake, Navy Pier

An oasis for urban outdoor enthusiasts in need of a quick fix, the northern lakefront is a Chicago gem. Starting on the North Side of Chicago at Ardmore-Hollywood Beach and extending clear down past the South Side's Chicago Cultural Center, this lakefront trail hugs the shoreline as it gently curves to the east.

Sunshine brings many joggers, walkers, in-line skaters, and bikers to its pavement. Repaired each year by the Chicago Park District from the wear and tear of winter, the pavement along the lakefront is often smooth unless under construction. Between Lake Michigan and Lake Shore Drive, you'll be immersed in trail, beach, green space, and harborfront. Often the name of the east-west street you're adjacent to is also the name of the beach, park, or harbor along the lakefront.

Between Foster Beach and Montrose Harbor, great grassy expanses are scattered with playgrounds, soccer fields, and basketball courts. The trail forks at Foster Avenue, with a small segment

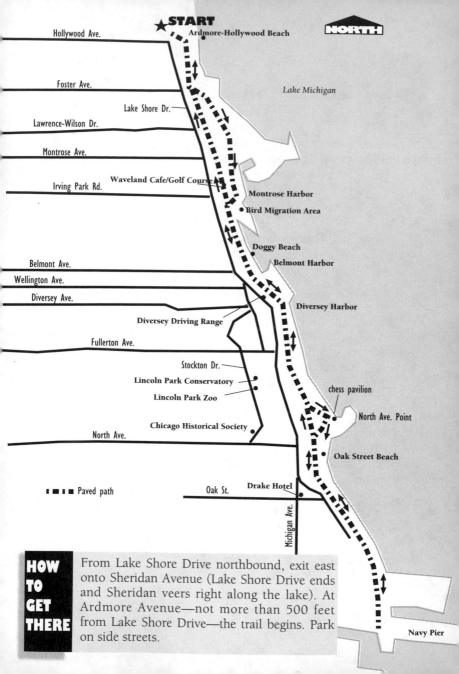

★ START
Ardmore-Hollywood Beach

Hollywood Ave.

NORTH

Foster Ave.

Lake Shore Dr.

Lawrence-Wilson Dr.

Montrose Ave.

Lake Michigan

Irving Park Rd.

Waveland Cafe/Golf Course

Montrose Harbor

Bird Migration Area

Doggy Beach

Belmont Ave.

Belmont Harbor

Wellington Ave.

Diversey Ave.

Diversey Harbor

Diversey Driving Range

Fullerton Ave.

Stockton Dr.

Lincoln Park Conservatory

Lincoln Park Zoo

chess pavilion

North Ave. Point

Chicago Historical Society

North Ave.

Oak Street Beach

Paved path

Oak St.

Drake Hotel

Michigan Ave.

Navy Pier

HOW TO GET THERE

From Lake Shore Drive northbound, exit east onto Sheridan Avenue (Lake Shore Drive ends and Sheridan veers right along the lake). At Ardmore Avenue—not more than 500 feet from Lake Shore Drive—the trail begins. Park on side streets.

0.0 Trail begins at intersection of Sheridan and Ardmore Avenues (5800 North Sheridan).

1.1 Pass Foster Avenue underpass. Parking available.

1.9 Pass Lawrence-Wilson Drive underpass.

2.2 Pass soccer fields on left.

2.5 Pass Montrose Harbor underpass.

3.1 Pass Irving Park Road underpass.

3.3 Pass Waveland Cafe.

3.4 Pass protected Bird Migration Area.

3.9 Pass Doggy Beach.

4.3 Pass Belmont Harbor underpass.

5.0 Pass Diversey Harbor underpass.

5.5 Pass Ranalli's Lakeside, Burritoville, Theater on the Lake.

6.3 Pass pedestrian overpass.

6.5 Pass chess pavilion, North Avenue underpass, Ed Debevic's.

7.4 Pass Oak Street Beach first-aid station.

8.7 Turn around at Navy Pier.

17.4 Return to your car on side streets along Ardmore Avenue.

of it heading out to the tip of the harbor—a good place for a breather.

South of Irving Park and right before Belmont Harbor, the trail curves around tennis courts and baseball diamonds. In the winter a section of the outfield is made into a small rink for ice skaters. On your left you'll see the fenced-in Bird Migration Protected Area. If you happen to be here at the right time of year, it'll teem with birds. This portion of the lakefront trail is less crowded, because it's farther north.

In the summer, beaches between Fullerton Avenue and North Avenue are strewn with volleyball nets and sunbathers. This portion of trail is often extremely crowded with adults and children walking out onto the path without looking. Be careful.

Farther south a chess pavilion, engraved with a large rook, encloses a series of chess boards laid in stone. The intrigue of speed chess often draws a small crowd of onlookers. At the pavilion, turn right and journey out to North Avenue Point for a spectacular view of the Chicago skyline.

Michigan Avenue begins on the other side of Lake Shore Drive at the famous Drake Hotel. When you reach the Drake, the trail shoots farther east, passing Oak Street Beach (adjacent to the prestigious Gold Coast neighborhood). Walk your bike through the first-aid station. Continue along the path on your way to the recently renovated Navy Pier, swarming with activity. To join in the festivities, lock your bike at the entrance. After a look at the sculpture garden and a stroll down the pier, mount up for your return.

Lakefront South

Number of miles:	25
Approximate pedaling time:	5 hours
Terrain:	Flat, well maintained
Traffic:	None
Things to see:	Lake Michigan, Museum Campus, harbors
Food and facilities:	Jackson Harbor Grill, Navy Pier, Museum Campus, Promontory Park, Jackson Harbor

East of Lake Shore Drive is the land of milk and honey. There's no better place for city dwellers who need to get away in a flash. Composed almost exclusively of lake and park, the southern lakefront takes you away from the city and almost everyone in it. Unlike the northern lakefront, which is often packed with people, the southern section offers solitude from the city.

Leaving the carousels and Ferris wheels of the Navy Pier carnival behind, the lakefront path crosses the Chicago River via a bridge that also serves lower Lake Shore Drive. Pedal up to get over it, then down back to the lakefront.

Scores of boats line Jackson Harbor, and across Lake Shore Drive squirts Buckingham Fountain at the center of Grant Park. Strong headwinds whirl and pedaling becomes fierce along an open straightaway. It's important that you become as aerodynamic as possible. A series of spaced-out museums known collectively as the Museum Campus comes into view.

Be prepared for a downhill leading toward Lake Michigan and the Shedd Aquarium. You can choose either to go around the

Shedd lakeside, or to ride through the Museum Campus to gaze at its ornate monumentality. The creation of this campus is recent and it was so big a project that it involved the re-routing of Lake Shore Drive. If you're a Chicago resident it's possible to get a pass from the library to see all three museums for free. This is a great place to stop if you have the time, and bike racks leave you little excuse not to go in for a peek.

The Shedd Aquarium is probably the most fun. Its celebration of marine life is apparent even in its exterior, which is adorned with seashells on the sides and a roof that looks like coral. If you decide to go in, splurge for the dolphin show; you won't be disappointed.

The shoreline pushes out eastward to form a peninsula at the site of the Adler Planetarium, whose dome-shaped roof is in fact a "Sky Theater." A 77-foot special-effects escalator brings you into the theater section. Live telescope viewings are offered at night, and indoor sky shows run during the day.

Also part of the campus is the Field Museum, the largest and most openly visible of the three buildings. Inside you'll find the biggest *T. rex* skeleton ever discovered, a re-creation of an Egyptian tomb, and replicas of the man-eating lions of Tsavo. The Museum Campus extends south to include Soldier Field, where the Chicago Bears play football and the Chicago Fire plays soccer.

Newer pavement is beneath you as the McCormick Place Convention Center approaches—so new that as of this writing, the asphalt is the only thing finished. The rest is dirt, still under construction. Crowds thin after McCormick Place, a horizontal behemoth whose design has been likened to Chicago's famous Prairie Style architecture. The trail runs next to the lake, with carefully placed trees lining its winding pathway.

You'll come upon older Chicago Park District buildings, some in better condition than others. The streets have become numbered by now. Beaches and harbors are spread sparsely as you continue southward. Stop for a break at Promontory Park. Look back

From the north, take Lake Shore Drive South (Route 41). Exit east at Grand Avenue and drive to Navy Pier. You'll find parking on the north side of the building.

90
94

Lake Shore Dr.

NORTH

Yacht Club

START

Navy Pier (parking)

Grant Park and Buckingham Fountain

Monroe Harbor

290

Roosevelt Rd.

Lake Michigan

Adler Planetarium

Soldier Field

Field Museum

McCormick Place

Shedd Aquarium

55

1st Street Beach

Pershing Rd.

Promontory Park

47th St.

Burnham Park

Museum of Science and Industry

Garfield Blvd.

Martin Luther King Dr.

63rd St. Beach House

Jackson Park

Jackson Grill

Marquette Rd.

Cultural Center

71st St.

Paved path

golf course

79th St.

94

90

DIRECTIONS
FOR
THE RIDE

0.0 Begin at Navy Pier parking lot.
0.3 Ride over bridge along lower Lake Shore Drive.
0.4 Pass Columbia Yacht Club on left.
1.8 Pass Museum Campus.
3.5 Pass Soldier Field.
4.5 Pass McCormick Place.
5.7 Pass 1st Street Beach and pedestrian overpass.
6.2 Pass another pedestrian overpass.
8.7 Pass fountain on right.
9.4 Pass Promontory Park.
9.8 Pass 57th Street Beach and Museum of Science and Industry.
10.6 Pass 63rd Street Beach House.
11.0 Pass Jackson Harbor Station and Jackson Harbor Grill.
11.5 Pass South Shore Cultural Center.
12.3 Pass golf course.
12.5 Turn around at 71st Street.
25.0 Return to Navy Pier parking lot.

to see the distant downtown skyscrapers that were once right in front of you.

You have left the city and immersed yourself in the lakefront. It's difficult to hear much more than your own breathing as the wind blows and waves crash into rocky shores. The trail ends with little notice at 7000 South, at the southern tip of the golf course. As you turn around to head north, hope for a tailwind.

6 Chain O' Lakes State Park

Number of miles:	6.2
Approximate pedaling time:	1½ hours
Terrain:	Flat, well maintained, paved
Traffic:	None
Things to see:	The Fox River
Food and facilities:	Concession stand south of Catfish Cove; rest rooms and picnic tables at Catfish Cove Picnic Area

The Chain O' Lakes bike path is a winding north–south ribbon linking three screened-limestone loops. It's well marked, well kept, and far removed from suburban surroundings. Ups and downs from the last receding glacier offer some vertical variety but, for the most part, this is an even-keeled ride through flora and forest. Ask nothing more of this trail and you'll go away happy.

The drive out to Chain O' Lakes is especially pleasant if you're coming from the city. This park is out there: country roads, small towns, little traffic. An occasional Harley reminds you that Wisconsin (the home of Harley-Davidson corporate headquarters) is no more than a short stretch of pavement away. Chain O' Lakes State Park is 4 miles south of the Illinois-Wisconsin border and just south of Lake Geneva—a Chicago-style version of New York's East Hampton, rife with summer cottages and quaint country shops. There's little question that this part of the state is a getaway from city swelter and suburban homogeneity. As you drive in through the park, notice that instead of a waterworld—which is what you'd expect with a name like *Chain O' Lakes*—you'll find

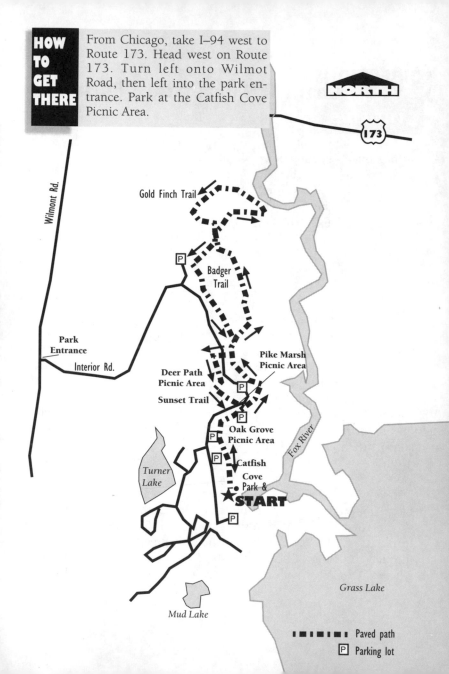

HOW TO GET THERE

From Chicago, take I–94 west to Route 173. Head west on Route 173. Turn left onto Wilmot Road, then left into the park entrance. Park at the Catfish Cove Picnic Area.

NORTH

173

Wilmont Rd.

Gold Finch Trail

P

Badger Trail

Park Entrance

Interior Rd.

Pike Marsh Picnic Area

P

Deer Path Picnic Area

Sunset Trail

P

Oak Grove Picnic Area

Fox River

P

Catfish Cove Park &

Turner Lake

P

★ START

P

Grass Lake

Mud Lake

■ ▪ ■ ▪ ■ ▪ ■ ▪ Paved path

P Parking lot

DIRECTIONS

FOR

THE RIDE

0.0 Turn right onto trail from Catfish Cove Picnic Area.

0.9 Pass Oak Grove turnoff.

1.2 Pass Pike Marsh Picnic Area. Turn right onto Sunset Trail.

1.9 Turn right onto Badger Trail.

3.1 Turn right onto Gold Finch Trail.

3.6 Pass parking lot.

3.8 Turn right onto Badger Trail.

5.0 Turn right onto Sunset Trail.

5.2 Pass Deer Path Picnic Area.

6.2 Return to Catfish Cove Picnic Area.

vegetation crowding a vast open prairie. Three natural lakes border the park, but most of what you see in the way of water here is lush marshland.

Bike rentals and concessions are located near the trailhead at Maple Grove. The trail winds its way northward through scattered tree trunks and open fields of brush that hide the many marshy wetland bogs swarming with marine activity. Signs indicate places to stop and venture out to observation decks. There's a ground-level wooden platform near the Pike Marsh Picnic Area that looks out onto a water basin covered with green algae.

When Europeans settled this area back in the 1600s, central Algonquin tribes such as the Miami, Mascouten, and Potawatomi grew corn, hunted, and fished while remaining semimobile throughout these parts. Though what little was left behind by Native Americans is now long gone, mature oak, hickory, cherry, spruce, and birch tree trunks remain from perhaps as far back as when the Civilian Conservation Corps (CCC) used this area as a camp in the 1930s.

As you reach the Sunset Trail, take the easterly route over a short bridge and experience a few mild hills. The Sunset Trail has the most humps in the park; still, you need to do little more than switch to a lower gear. Wildflowers are scattered through open fields, and signs indicate upcoming inclines, turns, and interior roadways.

What makes the "chain" in Chain O' Lakes is the Fox River, which links Grass Lake to Marie Lake to Nippersink Lake to Bluff Lake to Pistakee Lake to Channel Lake to Petite Lake to Catherine Lake to Redhead Lake. Made up of sixty-five hundred acres of water and 488 miles of shore, this string of water bodies—the largest grouping of natural lakes in Illinois—is locally known as the Fox Chain. Only on the northeastern portion of the trail will you ride along a stretch where the Fox River comes into view. As you continue up to and enter the Badger Trail, deep woods abound. The Fox River will be on your right.

Fox River North

Number of miles:	23.2
Approximate pedaling time:	6½ hours
Terrain:	Flat
Traffic:	Light
Things to see:	Fox River, wooden-planked bridge
Food and facilities:	Rest rooms and picnic tables at Fox River Shores Forest Preserve; eating establishments in the town of Elgin

From Twain's tales of the Mississippi to Marquette's historical foray down the Fox River's northerly stretch, rivers have long captivated the imagination of Americans. The Fox River Trail is the western suburbs equivalent to Chicago's lakefront. From Aurora on through to Algonquin, popping in and out of forest preserves, wooded areas, and townships, the Fox River Trail runs faithfully parallel to the Fox River throughout Kane County.

Originating as a right-of-way for two old train lines, the trail has since become so popular that talk of improvements include actually rerouting the Fox River to bring bikers farther into centers of towns. Expect a mostly paved and level surface with patches of limestone and few hills. The trail creeps up into towns at times but mostly remains furnished with sights of the Fox River from modest bluffs and shallow valleys. Temptation does knock as the well-marked path enters shopping areas in Elgin.

River and trail are in sight immediately as you enter the Blackhawk Forest Preserve parking lot—the start of this ride—and you'll notice a long bridge once you hit the trail. The boards stutter as you glide across 150 yards of river.

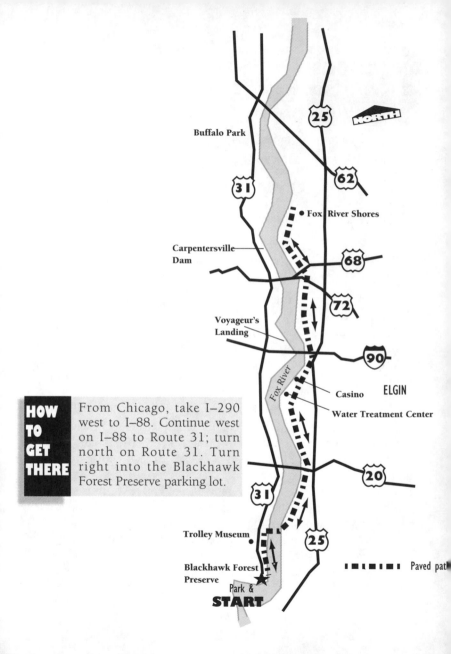

Buffalo Park

NORTH

25

62

31

Fox River Shores

Carpentersville
Dam

68

72

Voyageur's
Landing

90

ELGIN

Fox River

Casino

Water Treatment Center

HOW TO GET THERE From Chicago, take I–290 west to I–88. Continue west on I–88 to Route 31; turn north on Route 31. Turn right into the Blackhawk Forest Preserve parking lot.

31

20

Trolley Museum

25

Blackhawk Forest
Preserve

Park &
START

▪■▪▪■▪▪■▪ Paved pat

DIRECTIONS
FOR
THE RIDE

0.0 Turn left onto trail from Blackhawk
    Forest Preserve.
1.8 Cross Fox River.
4.0 Cross Route 20.
7.8 Cross I–90.

11.5 Turn around at Fox River Shores Forest Preserve.
13.0 Pass Carpentersville Dam.
16.6 Pass I–90.
23.2 Return to parking lot.

Don't forget bug spray if you plan on stopping frequently in wooded areas along the river. The tree-lined trail heading north out of the preserve is a well-shaded haven for mosquitoes. (A type of grape fern known as *Botrychium campaestre* was recently spotted here at the Blackhawk Forest Preserve—the first of its kind ever discovered in Illinois!)

After the preserve, you'll reach the Fox River Trolley Museum, which offers electric trolley car trips along the banks of the Fox River. Many antique trolleys run from lines that once connected Carpentersville, Elgin, Aurora, and Yorkville. In South Elgin, a bridge brings you to the eastern side of the river. On these winding trails—signed accordingly—rolling hills are a welcome challenge in an otherwise flat terrain.

The trail goes up through the side streets of Elgin, passing over railroad tracks and under a stone railroad bridge. At the Elgin Water Treatment Center, an elevated bluff view of the river offers a touch of exhilaration.

At the heart of the nation's dairy industry in 1860, Elgin's Board of Trade once set butter prices for the nation. These days the Grand Victoria Casino takes center stage in Elgin. Run by a partnership between Hyatt Development Corporation of Chicago and Circus Enterprises of Nevada, the casino is plopped down in the Fox River off Grove Street. Four hundred feet long, 114 feet wide, with 16-foot ceilings, the floating Grand Victoria can't be missed from the trail. Also within reach along the side streets of Elgin are quaint shops and cozy restaurants.

The forest swallows the trail again at Tyler Creek Forest Preserve, Fox River Shores, and Carpentersville. Tyler Creek, a shallow push of water running east, is frequented by the students of nearby Judson College. A hiking trail veers off to facilities on the western side of the river. After passing under I–90, find the historic millrace area known as Carpentersville Dam. This will soon have observation decks, hiking trails, and a boat launch.

Hyde Park

Number of miles:	6.8
Approximate pedaling time:	1½ hours
Terrain:	Flat, paved
Traffic:	Moderate
Things to see:	Museum of Science and Industry, University of Chicago campus, Robie House
Food and facilities:	Starbucks at campus bookstore, Museum of Science and Industry, and additional shops in the area

The main attractions in Hyde Park are the University of Chicago and the charming neighborhood that has built itself up around it, but the Museum of Science and Industry is nothing to scoff at. You'll notice its monumentality as you turn onto 57th Street but continue to be impressed inside: A 16-foot model of the human heart competes with a captured German submarine, an IMAX theater, and a simulated space shuttle ride. There are places to lock your bike, so make a pact with yourself or your companions to see the museum either before or after your ride.

To North Siders, taking a ride through Hyde Park is like lifting up the South Side shroud to reveal a pristine neighborhood of tree-lined streets and grey-slate architecture. Once you've passed under the elevated train, the University of Chicago campus promenade of stone architecture begins. Though a few more modern structures are intermingled, they take little away from the Old World character this school is known for. As you jut in and out of

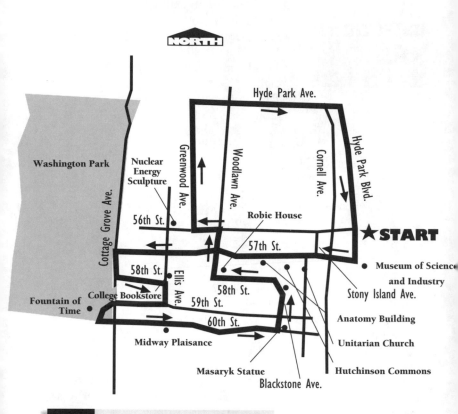

NORTH

Hyde Park Ave.

Washington Park

Greenwood Ave.

Woodlawn Ave.

Cornell Ave.

Hyde Park Blvd.

Nuclear
Energy
Sculpture

Robie House

Cottage Grove Ave.

56th St.

57th St.

★ **START**

● **Museum of Science
and Industry**

58th St.

Ellis Ave.

58th St.

59th St.

Stony Island Ave.

College Bookstore

Fountain of
Time ●

60th St.

Anatomy Building

Unitarian Church

Midway Plaisance

Masaryk Statue

Blackstone Ave.

Hutchinson Commons

**HOW
TO
GET
THERE**
From the north, take Lake
Shore Drive south (Route 41).
Get off at the 57th Street exit
and turn west. Park at the
Museum of Science and Indus-
try or on side streets.

0.0 Turn left out of the Museum of Science and Industry lot.

0.1 Cross Cornell Avenue.

0.2 Pass under trestle.

0.7 Pass First Unitarian Church (1836) on right.

0.8 Pass University of Chicago Hutchinson Commons on left.

0.9 Pass University of Chicago Biological Laboratories Anatomy Building.

1.3 Turn left onto Cottage Grove Avenue.

1.4 Turn left onto 58th Street.

1.6 Dead end at University of Chicago Bookstore and Starbucks restaurant. Turn right onto Ellis Avenue.

1.8 Turn right onto 59th Street. Turn left onto Cottage Grove. Turn right onto Midway Plaisance loop. Pass Fountain of Time sculpture. Turn right onto Cottage Grove.

2.5 Turn left onto 60th Street.

2.7 Pass map of University of Chicago campus.

3.5 Turn left onto Blackstone Avenue across park. Pass Masaryk statue.

3.8 Turn left onto 58th Street.

4.1 Pass Robie House.

4.2 Turn right onto Woodlawn Avenue.

4.4 Turn left onto 56th Street.

4.5 Pass the Smart Museum of Art.

4.7 Pass Nuclear Energy Sculpture (off Ellis Avenue). Turn around.

5.0 Turn left onto Greenwood Avenue.

5.5 Turn right onto Hyde Park Avenue.

6.2 Turn right onto Hyde Park Boulevard.

6.8 Return to Museum of Science and Industry.

side streets, notice the vintage charm of two- and three-flat residences built over a hundred years ago.

Little automotive traffic will interfere with your experience of this surprisingly unurban city campus. Aside from the area near the Fountain of Time sculpture, which sees high traffic, most streets are only busy with walking and biking students. It's best to keep your hands on the brakes and your eyes on lookout for pedestrians crossing.

Bordered by two narrow streets, the Midway Plaisance—a grassy rectangular hunk of lawn clustered with lounging students—acts as an unofficial quadrangle for the campus. At the head of the quad stands the Masaryk statue: a soldier on his horse charging forward. Bikes can be locked nearby along the same street as a Starbucks coffee shop, in the same building as a Barnes and Noble student bookstore.

Along a quiet street, near the great domed University of Chicago church, stands one of Frank Lloyd Wright's most famous houses. The Robie House was designed for a well-heeled inventor who designed bicycles in the Chicago area. Frederick C. Robie, who cruised around town in a prototype vehicle he designed himself, commissioned Wright for this project. Built on a low horizontal plane, much like the flat prairie landscape once typical throughout Illinois, the Robie House defined one of the first architectural styles to come out of America—the Prairie Style.

The best way to see Hyde Park is by bike, but even if you live on the North Side of Chicago, it's best to drive to Hyde Park first and then bike. Although Hyde Park is beautiful, it's separated from the downtown area and North Side by many less-than-desirable neighborhoods. Unless you choose to bike down along the lakefront, arrive here by car.

Lincoln Park Ride

Number of miles:	7.9
Approximate pedaling time:	2½ hours
Terrain:	Flat, paved
Traffic:	Moderate
Things to see:	Lincoln Park Zoo, Chicago Historical Society, Gold Coast and Old Town neighborhoods
Food and facilities:	Lincoln Park Zoo, Chicago Historical Society, Lincoln Park Conservatory, Diversey Driving Range

This ride brings you through some of the best parks just west of Lake Shore Drive. It also brings you through one of the most affluent areas in Chicago, the Gold Coast.

As you head south from Barry Avenue through what is known as Wellington Park, you'll notice that the trail is mostly paved with patches of limestone. There's light shade, with trees spread out. Bikers, dog walkers, in-line skaters, and joggers all frequent this trail because it's less crowded and arguably more pleasant than the lakefront. At the edge of the Diversey Driving Range a row of weeping willows hides the high fence. Once in a blue moon, a ball clears the fence, so be on the lookout.

The trail sinks down to avoid the Fullerton Avenue feed onto Lake Shore Drive. Just after the harbor, and before a boathouse standing flush with North Pond (often used for sculling) a steep decline takes you beneath the bridge.

Tree roots have bulged up along this older portion of pavement, making some patches bumpy but not unbearable. The trail sinks down once more under North Avenue, and you've entered the Gold Coast.

Some say the Gold Coast got its name because, in order to live here, you have to be made of gold—which is not too far from the truth. In 1880 the well-connected Palmer family decided to move here from Prairie Avenue, and many of their wealthy cohorts followed suit. The architecture along these streets warrants a ride slow enough for peeping. Gated gardens, luxurious terrace walkways, and unspeakably ornate interiors can be seen from the street.

To get a more complete sense of the Gold Coast and many other Chicago treasures, lock your bike and head into the Chicago Historical Society. If you haven't the time, then at least check out the wonderful flower garden just behind the society.

Old Town, just west and north of the Gold Coast, is probably the second most affluent area in the city, but its origins were quite different. Artists, writers, and other members of Bohemia settled Old Town in the 1960s, lining Wells Street with hip storefronts and cafes. Riding through present-day Old Town, you'll find an artsy ambience augmented by a series of cobblestone streets and alleys.

Your return trip is just as much a Chicago park treat, for you ride along Lincoln Park West (a street inside the park). This—not the neighborhood where all the young urban professionals live—is the real Lincoln Park. Though buses run through, there's less traffic along these streets, and a path pops up after the first few parking lots. The Lincoln Park Zoo and the Conservatory on the left are not to be missed.

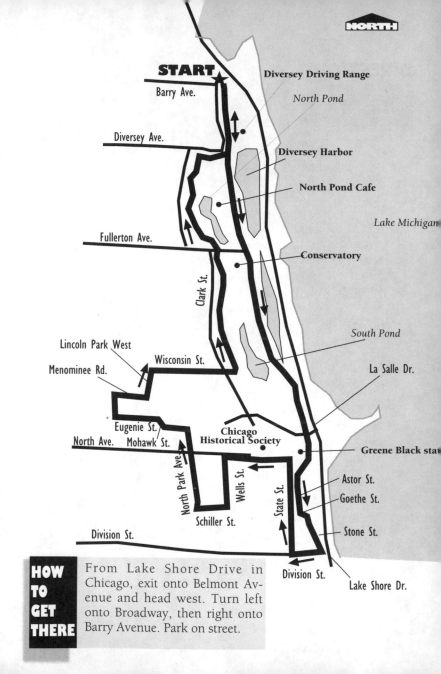

NORTH

START

Barry Ave.

Diversey Driving Range

North Pond

Diversey Ave.

Diversey Harbor

North Pond Cafe

Lake Michigan

Fullerton Ave.

Conservatory

Clark St.

South Pond

Lincoln Park West

Wisconsin St.

La Salle Dr.

Menominee Rd.

Eugenie St.

North Ave.   Mohawk St.

Chicago
Historical Society

Greene Black star

North Park Ave.

Wells St.

State St.

Astor St.

Goethe St.

Schiller St.

Stone St.

Division St.

Division St.

Lake Shore Dr.

HOW TO GET THERE From Lake Shore Drive in Chicago, exit onto Belmont Avenue and head west. Turn left onto Broadway, then right onto Barry Avenue. Park on street.

0.0 Turn right onto to path from Barry Avenue.

0.3 Pass Diversey Driving Range.

0.7 Pass Diversey Harbor Marina.

1.0 Pass under Fullerton Avenue.

1.7 Pass statue.

2.0 Pass lakefront walkover.

2.3 Pass under La Salle Drive access road. Turn left.

2.4 Trail curves right to Astor Street. Pass statue of Greene Black.

2.7 Astor Street jogs right.

2.8 Turn left onto Goethe Street.

2.9 Turn right onto Stone Street.

3.1 Turn right onto Division Street.

3.3 Turn right onto State Street.

3.8 Turn left onto North Avenue.

4.0 Pass Chicago Historical Society.

4.2 Turn left onto Wells Street.

4.5 Turn right onto Schiller Street.

4.6 Turn right onto North Park Avenue.

4.8 Cross North Avenue.

4.9 Turn left onto Concord Place.

5.0 Turn right onto Sedgwick Street.

5.1 Turn left onto Eugenie Street.

5.2 Turn right onto Mohawk Street.

5.4 Turn right onto Menominee Road.

5.5 Turn left onto Lincoln Park West.

5.7 Turn right onto Wisconsin Street.

5.8 Cross Clark Street. Turn left onto trail. Pass Lincoln Park Zoo.

6.3 Pass Lincoln Park Conservatory.

6.4 Pass Fullerton Avenue.

6.8 Pass North Pond Cafe.

7.2 Pass Diversey Harbor.

7.9 Return to Barry Avenue.

Deer Grove Preserve

Number of miles:	10.5
Approximate pedaling time:	3 hours
Terrain:	Paved and unpaved, with hills
Traffic:	None
Things to see:	Deer, prairie, forest
Facilities:	Rest rooms and drinking fountains throughout the preserve

Deer Grove comes in two flavors: open prairie paved, and deep woods unpaved. Both are hilly. A ride through each keeps those who know about Deer Grove coming back for more. As forest preserves go this one is a favorite because it's close to Chicago, easy to bike, and lots of fun. It's also one of the few mountain-biking trails available in Cook County that satisfies hill hunger without overwhelming you.

Though Deer Grove is not immense, it makes good use of the space it has without confusing switchbacks and interior loops. Signs mapping out the preserve and your location are a help when you're unsure how far you've gone. Though its suburban surroundings do little to inspire a feeling of isolation as you drive in, the eighteen hundred acres inside hide well what's outside.

A series of ravines feeds two lakes located within the preserve, but they are off limits. Erosion due to excessive trail blazing by mountain bikers and horseback riders has led Deer Grove management to urge visitors to stay on the existing trails. Hilly areas near the ravines that once sprawled with ground cover are now barren; once-undisturbed trees and shrubs are becoming undermined. A large orange sign near the ravines diagrams the severity of this ero-

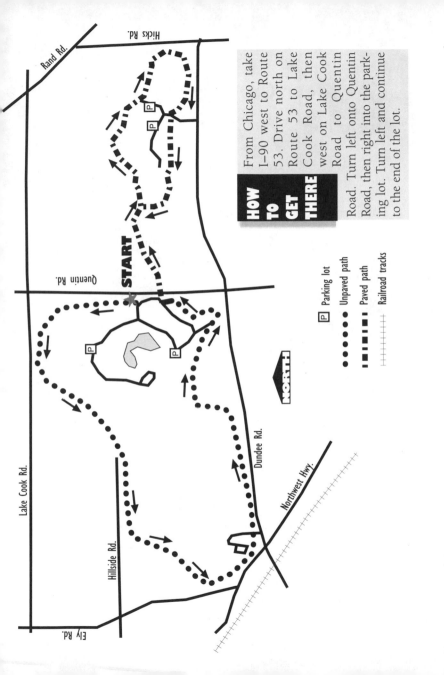

START

HOW TO GET THERE

From Chicago, take I-90 west to Route 53. Drive north on Route 53 to Lake Cook Road, then west on Lake Cook Road to Quentin Road. Turn left onto Quentin Road, then right into the parking lot. Turn left and continue to the end of the lot.

Rand Rd.

Hicks Rd.

Quentin Rd.

Lake Cook Rd.

Hillside Rd.

Ely Rd.

Dundee Rd.

Northwest Hwy.

NORTH

P Parking lot
• • • Unpaved path
▬ ▬ ▬ Paved path
+++++ Railroad tracks

DIRECTIONS

FOR

THE RIDE

0.0 Turn left out of parking lot onto un-
     paved trail.
1.8 Turn right at fork.
4.5 Turn left onto to paved trail at fork.
6.1 Cross Quentin Road.
6.6 Turn right at fork.
9.4 Turn right at fork.
9.9 Cross Quentin Road.
10.5 Return to parking lot.

sion. While riding on the unpaved portion, be sure to follow trail markers.

The unpaved section of this ride would only disappoint a mountain biker of advanced skill, though it's not too much for the average biker. Brilliant curves of dirt single track twist through the forest; you'll keep your hands ready for whatever is next!

Deer Grove's unpaved trails are also used by hikers, horseback riders, and, in the winter, cross-country skiers. It is important to stop and walk your bike should you come upon horseback riders. The sight of an oncoming bike will often spook even the most even-tempered breeds.

The paved portion of Deer Grove, located east of Quentin Road, has many modest inclines. You'll be in and out of forest for much of the trail, but the rest is restored open prairie. Deer often graze in these open fields, allowing for good photo opportunities. Bikers zoom in and out of the patches of forest into open fields and open skies. Somehow you forget about the world of houses and highways when you're amid this tall prairie grass and hills of dirt trail.

North Branch Trail

Number of miles:	11.6
Approximate pedaling time:	3 hours
Terrain:	Paved, a few hills
Traffic:	None
Things to see:	Toboggan slide, forest
Facilities:	Rest rooms and drinking fountains throughout the preserve

Though you could walk onto the North Branch Trail from any street it crosses, you'd be instantly within the natural confines of the forest preserve. This ride is very suburban but these are nice, low-key suburbs with few or no commercial buildings in sight. The trail stays within the woods, shooting straight north, following the North Branch of the Chicago River. Though you're occasionally reminded of where you are by the sight of cars as you peer through the trees, there's little but trail, river, and thick forest.

In the summertime Wealan Pool teems with kids jumping every which way; be careful driving in. To find the trailhead, just look for a brown 20-foot twin toboggan slide. A steep downhill of 50 feet starts you on your way through Clayton Woods, which is partially wooded with a grassy-park feel to it. As you pedal along, a dense forest closes in on the well-paved trail. It's not uncommon to see in-line skaters enjoying this smooth pavement while trying to avoid the small branches and wet patches along the trail. There are few occasions to shift up or down. Many of the streets you'll cross along the way are less than busy, though you will have to stop and push a button for traffic to stop on some of them.

The trail begins on the eastern side of the river but crosses to

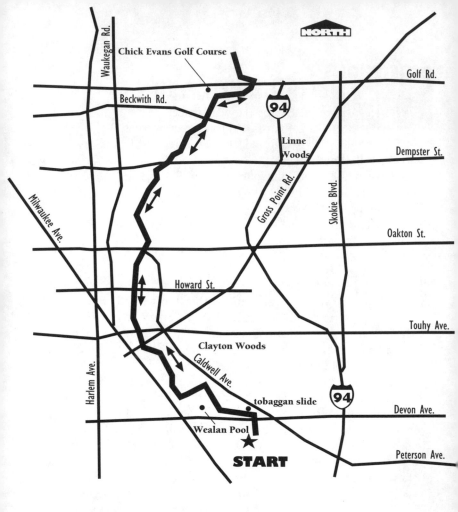

NORTH

Waukegan Rd.

Chick Evans Golf Course

Beckwith Rd.

Golf Rd.

94

Linne
Woods

Dempster St.

Gross Point Rd.

Skokie Blvd.

Milwaukee Ave.

Oakton St.

Howard St.

Touhy Ave.

Clayton Woods

Caldwell Ave.

Harlem Ave.

94

tobaggan slide

Devon Ave.

Wealan Pool

★
START

Peterson Ave.

HOW TO GET THERE From Chicago, take I–94 west to Route 14, then Route 14 north to Devon Avenue. Drive west on Devon Avenue to Wealan Pool. Turn right into the parking lot.

0.0 From Wealan Pool parking lot, find trail near toboggan slide.
1.0 Cross Gross Point Road.
1.2 Cross Touhy Avenue.
1.8 Cross Howard Street.
2.4 Cross Oakton Street overpass.
3.8 Cross Dempster Street.
4.8 Cross Beckwith Road.
5.0 Pass Chick Evans Golf Course.
5.8 Turn around at Golf Road.
6.8 Cross Beckwith Road again.
7.8 Pass Linne Woods again.
11.6 Return to parking lot.

the west at Touhy Avenue, then heads back east after the railroad tracks near the Morton Grove Train Station at Dempster. Though Skokie is popular, it's not so much a place where you'll stop a lot to look at attractions as it is a place to just take in, enjoying the overhanging trees and breezes of pavement riding. Though speed training is prohibited here, many bikers scoot along at a fast pace. The fall brings a great many leaves to the pavement; be careful when stopping or turning under these conditions.

The river is slow moving and appears deep. What's nice about this trail is that while you're not far from civilization, you're still experiencing the forest, exploring a snug corridor left uncarved by development. It's almost unimaginable that the entire surrounding landscape was once wooded and all that's left is this tight forest! Appreciation and enjoyment of the North Branch come quite naturally.

Old Plank Road Trail

Number of miles:	21.3
Approximate pedaling time:	4½ hours
Terrain:	Flat, paved
Traffic:	None
Things to see:	Farmland, Trolley Barn
Food and facilities:	Trolley Barn, Hickory Creek Park

Old Plank Road is for those who have long wanted to stop along those country roads lined with fields of wheat, corn, or beans to take it all in. It's for anyone who has ever become mesmerized by the gently curving rows of fields but never stopped to look up close, experiencing what farmers feel when they're out in the open, with the company of clouds and sky, tending to crops on a horizontal plane of land.

A trip out to the Plank Road Trail is a journey into Illinois farmland in the midst of new development. On the highway into town, I spotted a glittering evangelical billboard beside the road; it advertised a television show with the tag line WINNING IN LIFE and cornfields in the background. This is God's country for sure.

A trail bridge extends over Route 30, leading you to the main trail, which runs north–south. The trail curves southward where the construction of a paved northbound extension is under way. Phase II of development will bring the trail as far north as Joliet. In existence since 1980, the group that manages the trail includes one voting member from each town the trail passes through.

The trip down Plank Road Trail is a straight shot. Farmlands on the left, a few new houses on the right. Rows of gently rolling

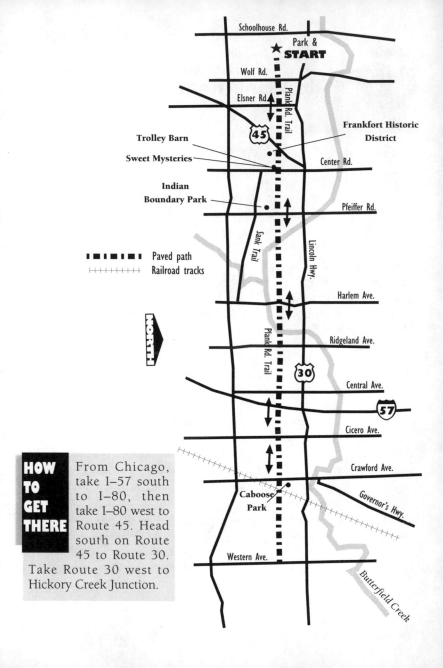

Schoolhouse Rd.

Park &
START

Wolf Rd.

Elsner Rd.

Plank Rd. Trail

45

Frankfort Historic District

Trolley Barn

Sweet Mysteries

Center Rd.

Indian Boundary Park

Pfeiffer Rd.

Sauk Trail

Lincoln Hwy.

■ ■ ■ ■ ■ ■ Paved path
┼┼┼┼┼┼┼┼┼ Railroad tracks

Harlem Ave.

NORTH

Plank Rd. Trail

Ridgeland Ave.

30

Central Ave.

57

Cicero Ave.

HOW TO GET THERE From Chicago, take I–57 south to I–80, then take I–80 west to Route 45. Head south on Route 45 to Route 30. Take Route 30 west to Hickory Creek Junction.

Crawford Ave.

Governor's Hwy.

Caboose Park

Western Ave.

Butterfield Creek

DIRECTIONS
FOR
THE RIDE

0.0 Trail begins 0.5 mile south of Hickory Creek Junction parking lot.
0.8 Cross Wolf Road.
3.0 Cross Elsner Road.
4.7 Cross Center Road. Pass Frankfort Historic District.
5.8 Cross Indian Boundary Park.
5.9 Cross Pfeiffer Road.
8.0 Cross Harlem Avenue.
11.1 Cross Cicero Avenue in commercial center of Matteson.
12.2 Turn around at Caboose Park.
16.2 Cross Harlem Avenue again.
21.3 Return to parking lot.

cornfields are at eye level. With no trees arching over the trail, you'll get a feeling of wide open space as you travel along this unwavering trail. You'll feel taller, as though you were on stilts and at odds with a vast horizon.

Miniature stop signs indicate an upcoming road, though you'll see little activity, let alone a place to stop for refreshments. Few travel these new roads, which bring with them new building construction. Route 45 is an exception, however, a long highway that hosts high-speed passersby.

Because the trail is in such good condition, it's used by bikers, in-line skaters, dog walkers, and even baby-stroller joggers. The trail runs right into the town center of Frankfort. An arched iron sign over the trail reads PLANK ROAD TRAIL, welcoming you to town. There are many places to lock your bike in the commercial center of Frankfort. At the Trolley Barn, antique maps of the area and remnants from the old railroad line that once ran along the Plank Road Trail decorate the walls. Stop in for a milk shake at Sweet Mysteries. And to take full advantage of your excursion into farm country, stop in at the fresh vegetable stand just before the highway on your way out of town.

Waterfall Glen

Number of miles:	8.5
Approximate pedaling time:	2 hours
Terrain:	Unpaved, some hills
Traffic:	None
Things to see:	Waterfall
facilities:	Rest rooms and water fountains near parking lots

At the glen, trails are 8 feet wide, white-tailed deer are plentiful, and a scattering of pine groves planted long ago by the federal government offers constant changes in color and composition. Though some bikers pedal along at a fast pace, you'll find here a level of courtesy that's not always present on mountain-bike-friendly preserves. Less rugged than Cook County's neighboring trails of Palos (see ride 25) and Sag Valley (see ride 36), Du Page County's Waterfall Glen is suited for bikers of all shapes and sizes.

I'd be hard pressed to offer a ride comparable to Waterfall Glen. At the nucleus of the glen is the Argonne National Laboratory, one of the largest federally funded research facilities in physical, biomedical and environmental sciences, and in the development of energy sources for the future. Though little more than parking lots and signage give you an indication that a laboratory sits within this preserve, your curiosity may be aroused as to exactly what you're biking around.

Manageable hills are common here, and green grass fire lanes off limestone trails offer great places to turn off for a picnic on gentler grounds. It's difficult to know how many people are on the trail until you get in, due to its twist and turns and to the multiple

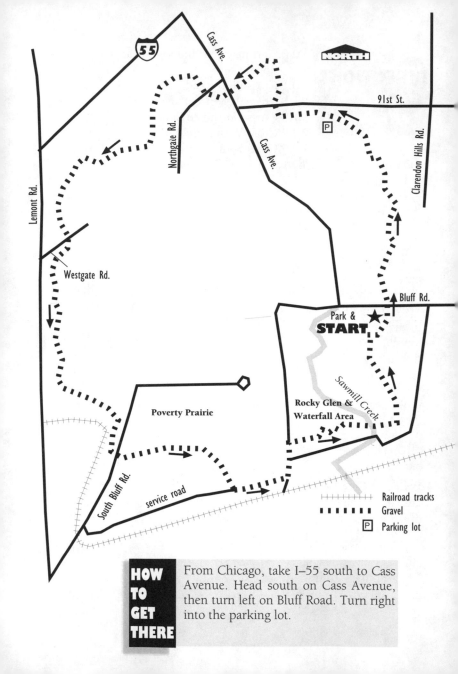

55

Cass Ave.

NORTH

91st St.

Northgate Rd.

Cass Ave.

Clarendon Hills Rd.

Lemont Rd.

P

Cass Ave.

Westgate Rd.

Bluff Rd.

Park &
START

Sawmill Creek

Poverty Prairie

**Rocky Glen &
Waterfall Area**

South Bluff Rd.

service road

++++++++++ Railroad tracks
∎∎∎∎∎∎∎∎∎∎ Gravel
P Parking lot

HOW TO GET THERE

From Chicago, take I–55 south to Cass Avenue. Head south on Cass Avenue, then turn left on Bluff Road. Turn right into the parking lot.

DIRECTIONS

FOR

THE RIDE

0.0 Start near parking lot entrance at Educational Camp.

0.1 Cross Bluff Road.

1.5 Cross 91st Street again.

1.8 Cross Northgate Road.

3.7 Cross Westgate Road.

5.5 Cross South Bluff Road.

6.3 Ride along service road.

7.3 Return to trail.

7.5 Cross Sawmill Creek.

7.9 Pass waterfall area.

8.5 Return to parking lot.

parking places around the preserve. Trails do cross suburban roads that you should be wary of, but most of the time traffic is minimal

Waterfall Glen is the largest forest preserve in Du Page County. It has long been known of, even before bikers buzzed through its forest. Though trails are now well maintained and well wooded, this was not always the case. In the 1860s the Ward Brothers' sawmill cranked out a fair share of lumber from this land; later, Edwin Walker is known to have supplied the limestone that went into the Chicago Water Tower out of a quarry once in the glen.

Along the southeastern portion of this trail, you'll spot—amid tree branches and slate rocks—the waterfall the preserve is *not* named after. Created in the 1930s by the Civilian Conservation Corps, an impressive 10-foot waterfall that many associate with Waterfall Glen lies just off the trail. Oddly enough, though, Waterfall Glen is named for Seymour "Bud" Waterfall, an early president of the district board of commissioners.

Bong State Recreation Area

Number of miles:	7.2
Approximate pedaling time:	3½ hours
Terrain:	Grassy fairways, many mild hills
Traffic:	None
Things to see:	Wolf Lake, tall grass
Food and facilities:	Mars Cheese Castle; also rest rooms and water fountains near parking lots of Bong State

Just past the Wisconsin-Illinois border, Bong is one of the closest Wisconsin escapes for Chicagoland bikers. Compared to the largely flat topography and suburban surroundings of Chicagoland, many Chi-towners rightly consider Wisconsin a wilderness state with its rivers, backcountry, and even mountain getaways. Though there are no mountains and few rivers or backcountry at Bong State Recreation Area, it is a refreshing chunk of wilderness. To get a sense of what's in store for you, while there are 4,515 acres of land at Bong, only 6 percent is intensely developed. Wide grass trails run through open prairie amid tall swamp grass and open fields. A few mild climbs and the absence of nearby facilities aside, this is a trail many manage easily.

Just off the I-94 exit is Mars Cheese Castle, a great stop on your way out of Dodge. It has all the beer, brats, and Wisconsin cheese anyone could ever want. It's also a German deli, a tavern, and a souvenir shop. Being in Wisconsin, the state famous for cheese, a stop here is like paying homage.

You can count on Wisconsin to be a little cooler than Chicago,

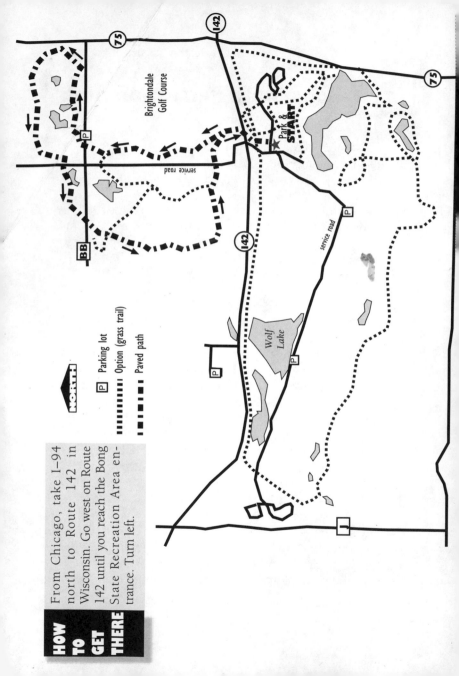

HOW TO GET THERE

From Chicago, take I–94 north to Route 142 in Wisconsin. Go west on Route 142 until you reach the Bong State Recreation Area entrance. Turn left.

NORTH

P Parking lot

▪▪▪▪▪▪ Option (grass trail)

▪ ▪ ▪ ▪ Paved path

Brightondale Golf Course

service road

Park & START

Wolf Lake

service road

142

75

BB

0.0 Find trail at western corner of parking lot.
0.2 Cross Route 142.
0.3 Pass Pond.
0.5 Take right fork.
0.7 Take right fork.
1.5 Again, take right fork.
1.7 Cross Highway BB.
3.7 Take right fork.
4.5 Cross Highway BB.
5.1 Take right fork.
6.3 Take right fork.
6.6 Cross service road.
6.8 Take right fork.
6.9 Take right fork.
7.0 Cross Route 142.
7.2 Return to parking lot.

even though it's hardly an hour away (barring traffic). Park at the trail head lot after going through a manned booth. You'll have to pay $3.00 for a trail pass and $7.00 to park.

Bong State Recreation Area is named for Richard Ira Bong, a World War II ace fighter pilot born in Poplar, Michigan. The sign on the way in reads LARGEST MANAGED PRAIRIE, though this return to nature didn't originally come about for conservation purposes. Bong State Recreation Area was cleared in the 1950s by the U.S. government for a proposed military base that never came to be. Though much has grown since then, you'll notice a lack of trees while on the trail.

The parking lot sets the scene for what's to come—tall grass surrounds a marshy pond. As you cross the road you came in on, you'll see the Brightondale Golf Course is on your right, then never spot it again on your ride. The whole trail is grass, which seems to be regularly cleared so that branches don't creep in. While it may sound easy to ride on grass, it slows you down a bit, and in some places the trail surface gets bumpy.

What's special about Bong is that it was created for uses state parks and forests often don't accommodate (such as all-terrain mountain biking). Other activities at Bong include dog training, hot-air ballooning, hang gliding, hunting, trapping, and falconry. Though you may be tempted to explore the trails around large Wolf Lake, the better trails extend into the northern portions of the park. The best time to go is spring or summer. After the leaves fall and the grounds turn wet, leafy trails get slippery. And on sunny days, the lack of shade may take more out of you than you'd expect.

Kettle Moraine South

Number of miles:	7.3
Approximate pedaling time:	3½ hours
Terrain:	Very hilly, dirt
Traffic:	None
Things to see:	Mountainous terrain
Food and facilities:	La Grange General Store; rest rooms and water fountain at trail entrance

Kettle Moraine south is the most rigorous of the trails I cover in this book. For Chicagoland mountain bikers, it's the nearest taste of what real Wisconsin mountain biking is all about. Part of Kettle Moraine is the John Muir Trail, the best of breed for local mountain biking. It's also quite crowded on weekends.

The drive out to Kettle Moraine takes a turn for the better as soon as you turn off I–94: You leave behind the land of condominiums and overcrowded suburbs, and farm country kicks in. At the intersection of Highway H and Greening Road, just before you reach the trail, you'll come upon a corner store that doubles as a bike shop. Pick up a free trail map inside and you're sure to stop in afterward. Sandwiches are made with croissants, an assortment of fresh salads is in the deli case, and everything from bottled water to beer is in the fridge.

Before you hit the trail, be sure to pay for your parking permit ($7.00) and trail pass ($3.00). Though it looks like a measly little parking lot, park officials frequently roam the trails and outer limits of the park. A brown wooden sign offers a carved, color-coded rendition of the trail loops.

As you head out onto the trail, you'll have no choice but to

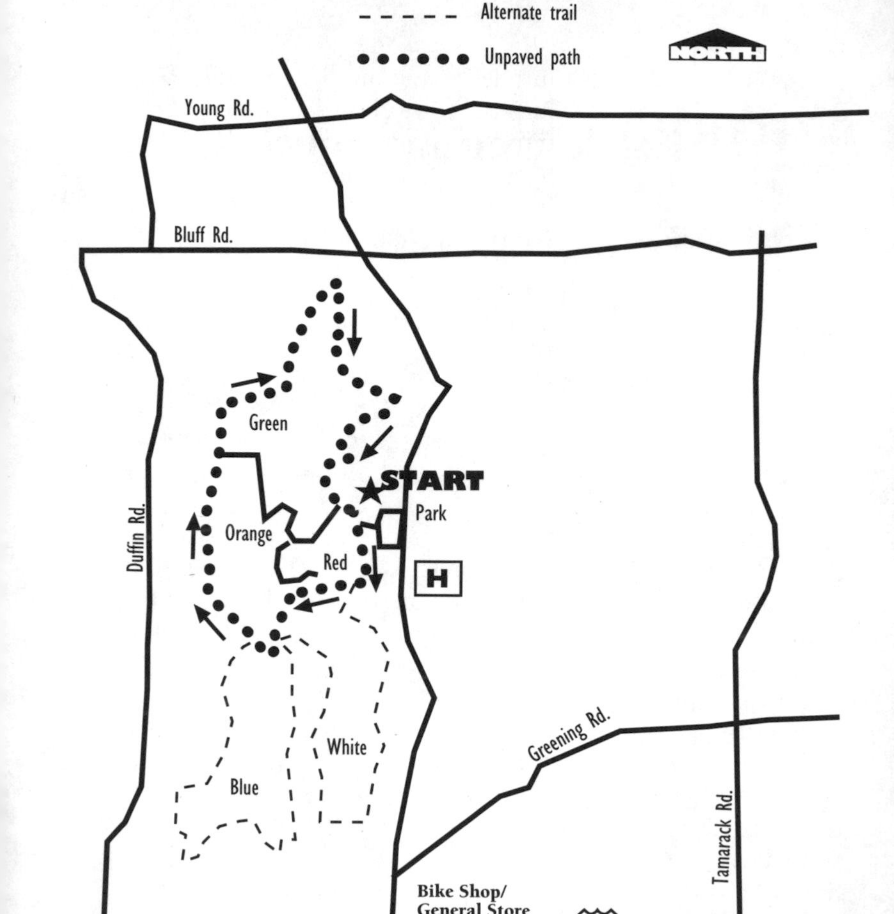

Alternate trail
Unpaved path

NORTH

Young Rd.

Bluff Rd.

Green

Orange

Red

START

Park

H

White

Blue

Duffin Rd.

Greening Rd.

Tamarack Rd.

Bike Shop/
General Store

12

HOW TO GET THERE From Chicago, take I–94 west to Route 50 in Wisconsin. Go west on Route 50 to Route 12. Turn north on Route 12 and drive to Route 67. Take Route 67 to Greening Road and turn right, then turn right again onto Highway H. Turn left into the parking area.

0.0 Turn left onto trail. Follow red loop.
0.7 Turn right at fork to stay on red loop.
1.4 Turn left at fork onto orange loop.
4.4 Turn left at fork onto green loop.
6.9 Turn left at fork onto red loop.
7.3 Return to parking lot.

turn left regardless of which loop you've chosen. Notice the series of colors marking the trails. Trail signage starts out with all colors showing; gradually your options narrow as you proceed. I've chosen a ride that starts on the red loop, then orange, then green, then red again. This will give you a taste of each trail type.

The first few miles along the red loop are a cinch. There are views of open prairie, some forest area, and a relatively smooth terrain. As you hit the inside portion of the orange loop, things get a bit more difficult; you may find yourself at odds with a few steep hills and some plastic-tread terrain (this plastic stuff is used to help save certain areas from erosion). Once you arrive at the green loop, be prepared for steep inclines and rocky trails. If it's too much, there's no shame in walking your bike down or up extreme slopes. The green trail is mostly single track and the most tumultuous toward the end. Note: A bike with shocks or some sort of suspension system may be in order, though I've ridden Kettle Moraine many times without either. A helmet is also important.

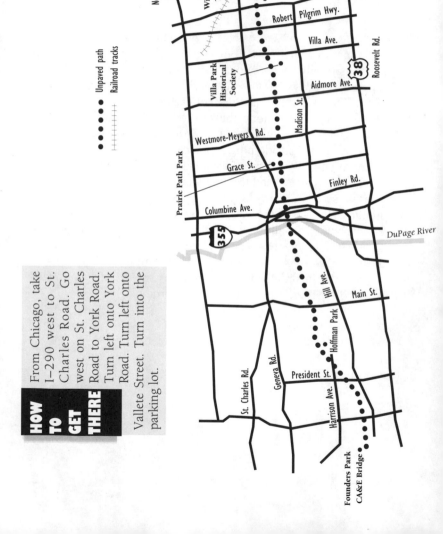

NORTH

START

Park & Vallede St.

St. Charles Rd.

York Rd.

North Rd.

64

Wild Meadows Trace Park

Spring Rd.

Robert Pilgrim Hwy.

Villa Ave.

Roosevelt Rd.

38

Villa Park Historical Society

Aidmore Ave.

Madison St.

Westmore-Meyers Rd.

Prairie Path Park

Grace St.

Finley Rd.

Columbine Ave.

355

DuPage River

Hill Ave.

Main St.

Hoffman Park

St. Charles Rd.

Geneva Rd.

President St.

Harrison Ave.

Founders Park

CA&E Bridge

• • • • Unpaved path
+++++++ Railroad tracks

HOW TO GET THERE

From Chicago, take I-290 west to St. Charles Road. Go west on St. Charles Road to York Road. Turn left onto York Road. Turn left onto Vallete Street. Turn into the parking lot.

Illinois Prairie Path

Number of miles:	20.6
Approximate pedaling time:	4 hours
Terrain:	Flat, limestone
Traffic:	None
Things to see:	Bridges, Founders Park
Food and facilities:	Food can be found in Weaton; rest rooms and water fountains at parks along the way

For those of you who cherish the presence of trails wherever they may be, the Illinois Prairie Path must be ridden out of respect for its origins. It's among the first large-scale rails-to-trails undertakings in the country. It all started with a letter published by the *Chicago Tribune* that took the form of a detailed proposal to convert an abandoned rail line into a pleasant trail for walking and biking. Mrs. May Theilgaard Watts, a noted author and environmentalist of the 1960s, wrote this letter and later started the Illinois Prairie Path Corporation (IPP).

Nowadays the path has a main stem, a north branch, a south branch, and two spurs, all coming out of Wheaton. This trail is straight and flat, good for a self-regulated ride. It's a trail that's been forgotten by most so, for weekenders, it's still a good place to get away from crowds.

There are many places to park along the way because of the many old train station stops. The train line that ran along this path was electric and ran from Chicago to Aurora to Elgin (CA&E). It was considered an "interurban" line. Starting in Elmhurst, the Illinois Prairie Path runs through a series of towns, crossing streets

DIRECTIONS

FOR

THE RIDE

0.0 Turn left out of parking lot.
0.5 Pass Wild Meadows Trace Park.
2.0 Pass Villa Park Historical Society.
4.2 Pass Prairie Path Park.
4.4 Pass Main Street.
7.7 Pass Elmer J. Hoffman Park.
10.3 Turn around at CA&E bridge at Illinois Prairie Path Volunteer Park.
14.5 Pass Route 355.
20.6 Return to parking lot.

and going through parking lots, but little trace of the railways remain. Instead, yellow dividers impede cars from trying to access the trail.

A few miles past Wild Meadows Trace Park in Elmhurst, the first patch of restored prairie (managed by local volunteers) flourishes on each side of the trail, which includes an interpretive garden. In the summer signs indicate the different kinds of prairie plants.

Farther along, in the town of Villa Park, an old train station houses the Villa Park Historical Society near the starting point of the Great Western Trail (another old train line turned trail; see ride 22).

As you near Route 355, get ready for a short uphill crank up to a bridge over Routes 355 and 53. Another bridge crossing the Du Page River is on the horizon.

You ride into the center of Wheaton, a small, charming college town with some hustle and bustle. Once you're past the existing Metra line, wildflowers shield you from in-town activities. Before returning to your car, check out Volunteer Park, where a large boulder stands behind words spoken by Watts: FOOTPATHS ARE DEFENDED WITH SPIRIT BY THEIR USERS.

Salt Creek Trail

Number of miles:	12.5
Approximate pedaling time:	2½ hours
Terrain:	Paved, mostly flat
Traffic:	None
Things to see:	Brookfield Zoo, Salt Creek
Food and facilities:	Brookfield Zoo

Aside from having no hills, Salt Creek is one of the best trails in Cook County. The surrounding suburbs are beautifully sculpted. It's the sort of perfect community you might want to raise your children in. The trail along Salt Creek starts between Oak Brook and Hinsdale, reaching up into La Grange and ending in Brookfield.

Salt Creek is a winding, paved trail that's a little older than most others in the county, but it has the right touch of charm. It's forested almost the entire way. At some points backyards sleeve the path on both sides. In other places the trail meanders alongside slow-moving Salt Creek. But best of all, at the far end of the ride is the Brookfield Zoo.

Within the first few miles, you'll find a few opportunities to head onto off-road single track that is hillier, but this portion of the trail is unmarked and a bit confusing. For the first half of the trail, Salt Creek stays to your right after you cross Wolf Road (here, on the other side of Salt Creek, is the Salt Creek Nursery). In warmer months Salt Creek is used by kayakers and canoers despite its shallow appearance. After Mannheim Road the creek stays on your left for a spell.

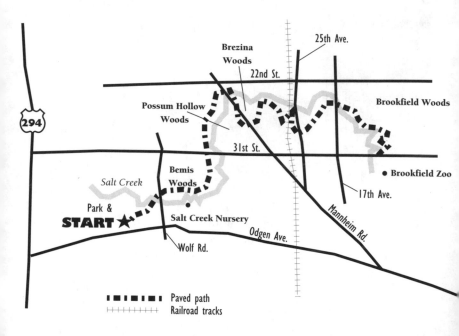

25th Ave.

Brezina
Woods

22nd St.

Possum Hollow
Woods

Brookfield Woods

294

31st St.

Salt Creek

Bemis
Woods

Brookfield Zoo

Park &
START ★

Salt Creek Nursery

17th Ave.

Mannheim Rd.

Odgen Ave.

Wolf Rd.

■ ■ ■ ■ ■ ■   Paved path
+++++++++   Railroad tracks

HOW TO GET THERE From Chicago, take I–290 west to I–294. Drive south on I–294 to Ogden Avenue (Route 34). Take Ogden Avenue east to Bemis Woods. Turn right into Bemis Woods where there is a parking lot.

DIRECTIONS

FOR

THE RIDE

0.0 Trail begins after first parking area in Bemis Woods South.

0.5 Cross Wolf Road.

1.9 Cross 31st Street. Enter Possum Hollow Woods.

2.0 Cross Mannheim Road. Enter Brezina Woods.

2.4 Cross interior parking lot.

4.3 Enter railroad underpass.

4.5 Cross 25th Avenue.

5.3 Pass 17th Avenue.

6.7 Enter Brookfield Woods parking lot.

6.8 Cross 31st Street to Brookfield Zoo. Turn around.

9.4 Cross Mannheim Road again.

12.5 Return to Bemis Woods parking lot.

There's little to distinguish one wooded area from the next aside from the names—Bemis Woods, Possum Hollow Woods, Brezina Woods, Westchester Woods, and Brookfield Woods. Toward the end of the trail, the forest opens up to small field of flowers and hooks around through a parking lot and past a rest home. Across busy 31st Street is the Brookfield Zoo.

Boasting 150 species of mammals, 125 species of birds, 120 species of reptiles and amphibians, and 20 species of invertebrates, the Brookfield Zoo offers a safari tour bus that visits its twenty naturalistic exhibits. You can either take a rest and let someone else take the wheel for a change or wander around on foot within the zoo's 216 acres. Just north of the trail in Brookfield is a school, so don't be surprised to see teenagers taking advantage of trail and zoo with you.

Great River Trail

Number of miles:	26.8
Approximate pedaling time:	6 hours
Terrain:	New pavement, some hills
Traffic:	None
Things to see:	Albany Indian Mounds, Mississippi River
Food and facilities:	Restaurants are located in Fulton and Albany; rest rooms available at the Fulton Rest Area near 11th Avenue and at the Albany Indian Mounds

For us Chicagoans who turn cold shoulders west while gazing onto a Great Lake that competes in character with the oceans beside the cities of the Atlantic and Pacific coasts, it's easy to forget that the Mississippi River runs along the entire western Illinois border. Residents of Fulton, a small river town on the border of Illinois and Iowa, certainly cannot forget the Mississippi, however. Faithfully following this great wide river as it winds its way southward, brand spankin' new pavement climbs hills and dips into valleys. If you're looking for a complete change in scenery, and willing to drive due west, the Great River Trail makes for a rewarding day or overnight trip. Not only can you experience a pleasant ride away from a thickly packed Chicago lakefront, but an early-evening ride offers the prospect of watching the sun set over the Mississippi (as it could never over Lake Michigan from Chicago).

The Great River Trail will bring you from Fulton to Albany. Some portions of the trail are in fact shared use, but it remains well marked. The start of the trail looks out on Lock & Dam 13,

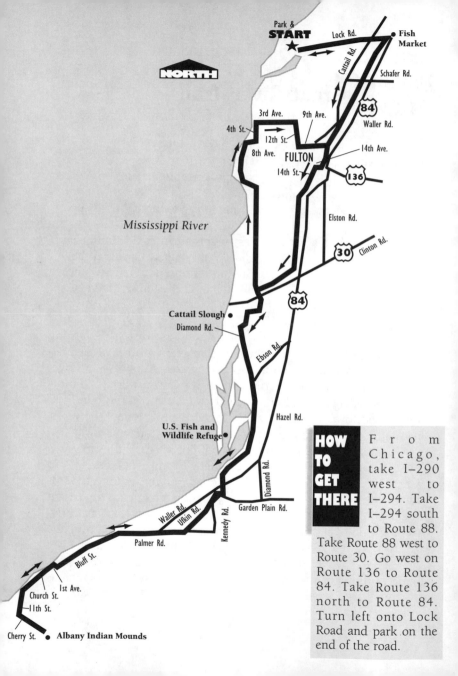

NORTH

Park &
START

Lock Rd.

● **Fish Market**

Cattail Rd.

Schafer Rd.

84

Waller Rd.

3rd Ave.   9th Ave.

4th St.

12th St.

8th Ave.   14th Ave.

FULTON

14th St.

136

Mississippi River

Elston Rd.

30   Clinton Rd.

84

Cattail Slough ●

Diamond Rd.

Ebson Rd.

Hazel Rd.

**U.S. Fish and
Wildlife Refuge** ●

Diamond Rd.

Waller Rd.   Ufkin Rd.

Kennedy Rd.

Garden Plain Rd.

Palmer Rd.

Bluff St.

1st Ave.

Church St.

11th St.

Cherry St. ● **Albany Indian Mounds**

HOW TO GET THERE From Chicago, take I–290 west to I–294. Take I–294 south to Route 88. Take Route 88 west to Route 30. Go west on Route 136 to Route 84. Take Route 136 north to Route 84. Turn left onto Lock Road and park on the end of the road.

0.0 Trail starts on Lock Road—a shared-use road.

1.7 Turn left at Schafer's Fish Market onto a paved trail.

4.6 Turn right onto 14th Avenue, a shared-use road, in Fulton.

4.7 Turn left onto 14th Street.

4.8 Return to paved trail.

6.6 Return to shared-use road.

7.3 Return to paved trail.

7.6 Trail turns to limestone.

9.0 Return to shared-used road. Turn right onto Palmer Road.

9.6 Turn left onto Bluff Street.

10.3 Turn right onto 1st Avenue then left onto Church Street.

10.5 Turn left onto 11th Street.

11.3 Return to paved trail.

12.7 Turn around at Albany Indian Mounds.

18.9 Turn left at a fork on paved trail along dike.

20.2 Turn right onto 8th Avenue. Trail returns to shared-use road.

20.6 Turn left onto 4th Street.

20.7 Turn right onto 3rd Avenue.

21.0 Turn right onto 12th Street.

22.2 Turn left onto 9th Avenue.

22.4 Return to paved trail.

25.1 Turn left onto Lock Road. Trail returns to shared-use road.

26.8 Return to parking lot.

one of about ten locks along the Illinois border. As you ride away from the water on the road you drove in on, signs indicate the right turn onto the trail just after an old fish market. The paved trail is very smooth and very new. You won't get a good view of the water for a bit, but this is a good way to ease into the ride. Shift to an appropriate gear and just coast along, taking care not to overexert too early.

As the Mississippi River comes into view, you'll find that you're at least 30 feet above the water for most of the trip; when you cross the bridge, the trail shoots down and then up again. After record high water brought a flood into Fulton in 1965, an extensive levee system was created that elevates this land high above the Mississippi.

After you cross the second bridge, a swampy patch of water indicates you've passed the Cattail Slough and soon after, the U.S. Fish and Wildlife Refuge. The trail veers away from the water, and then back near the shore as you approach the small commercial center of Albany. Not so long ago both Albany and Fulton received tons of river traffic and business from steamboats and log rafts. Fulton's football team, in fact, is named the Steamers in honor of days past. Albany, the site of a Hopewell Indian burial ground located at the southern tip of this trail, was also home to more than thirty riverboat captains, including Stephen H. Hanks, first cousin to Abraham Lincoln. As you ride through Albany, antiques stores with prices you won't find in the big city are tempting.

I & M Canal State Trail

Number of miles:	11
Approximate pedaling time:	2 hours
Terrain:	Flat, paved
Traffic:	None
Things to see:	I & M Canal
Food and facilities:	Corner store near park entrance

The entire stretch of the I & M Canal State Trail is 61 miles. It runs from Joliet to La Salle, though some parts are just for hiking. The portion in Joliet and closest to Chicago is a popular after-work ride during warmer months.

The tale of the I & M Canal is worth recounting. By linking the Great Lakes to the Illinois River, the creation of the I & M Canal forged a trade route between the eastern seaboard and mid-America. It was first observed by explorers Jolliet and Marquette that "half a league of prairie" (that's about 1.5 miles) came between an inland waterway running from the Atlantic Ocean to the Gulf of Mexico.

Here's how it works. The Great Lakes are connected to the Atlantic through the St. Lawrence Seaway, which shoots northwest off Lake Ontario. By way of Lake Erie and Lake Huron, you can travel by boat from Lake Ontario to Lake Michigan and enter the Chicago River, which then runs south through what are now Chicago suburbs. What was missing before the canal was built was a link from the Chicago River to the Des Plaines River, which then runs into the Illinois River, and then to the Mississippi River, which brings you down to the Gulf of Mexico.

Once you're off I–55 the green forest pleasantries hide the river

HOW TO GET THERE
From Chicago, take I–55 west to Willow Springs Road, then turn south on Willow Springs Road. Make two quick right turns after the railroad tracks. Turn left into the parking lot.

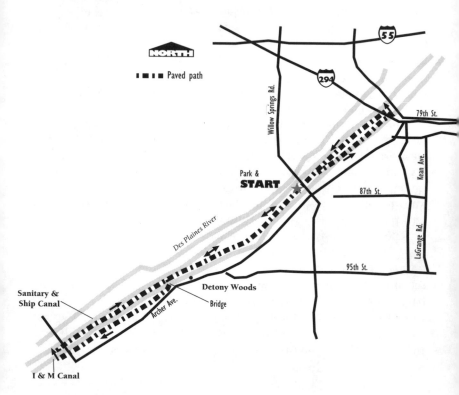

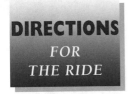

DIRECTIONS
FOR
THE RIDE

0.0 Turn right out of parking lot.
3.4 Return to parking lot. Pick up trail on
    other side.
5.6 Pass Henry Detony Woods.
9.1 Return to Henry Detony Woods.
11.0 Return to parking lot.

corridor from the road. You'll pass the Des Plaines River and the Sanitary & Ship Canal before you reach the I & M. Parking is a snap and the trail is not 50 paces away. This portion of trail consists of two loops, with the parking lot located close to dead center. Head out in the direction of the overpass. On the other side of the canal, the railroad tracks that once helped retire the canal from its commercial use are still in operation. Though the river originally triggered the presence of nearby canal towns, faster railroad transport drastically altered canal use around the late 1800s.

The first loop of the trail is a bit shorter and in better condition. As the path twists and turns, the canal comes in and out of view. Be on the lookout for slow-moving walkers behind bends. You know you've reached far end of the first loop when you pass under I–294. The return trip brings you along a later addition known as the Sanitary & Ship Canal. Once you hit the lot on your return, you're a little over one-third done.

The next phase of your trip is along the straight but not narrow. Cross the canal at Henry Detony Woods to ride along the train tracks for a spell before you reach the farthest stretch of the second loop. On the other side of the Route 83 underpass, cross back over and ride between the Sanitary & Ship Canal and the I & M. The last leg of your journey is even straighter. If you've still got it in you, here is the time to perspire or cherish your last sight of trees and water on each side.

Skokie Trail

Number of miles:	16.8
Approximate pedaling time:	3 hours
Terrain:	Paved, mostly flat
Traffic:	None
Things to see:	Skokie Lagoons, Chicago Botanical Gardens
Food and facilities:	Restaurant at Chicago Botanical Gardens; rest rooms and water fountains near trail's parking lots

Anyone who knows the Chicago suburbs will tell you that the Skokie Trail is something for suburbanites to be proud of. The trail runs through the North Shore towns of Glenview, Northfield, Northbrook, Glencoe, Winnetka, and Wilmette. While you're on the trail, however, little more than a few residential houses peek through.

The dark asphalt trail runs straight north through Blue Star Memorial Woods, Glenview Woods, and Harms Woods, then to the Skokie Lagoons, and on up to the Chicago Botanical Gardens. Talk about a great green oasis! And by the time you hit the botanical gardens, you may have turned green yourself: Fence-lined trails, long stretches of pavement, and dense forest shade make for some of the best flat-surface riding in Chicagoland. Though speed training is not permitted, this is a trail you can really haul through.

At the start of the trail, glimpses of the Chick Evans Golf Course can't be avoided. This portion of trail is the least crowded and, as you move farther along, the scenery gets better and the trail a bit more populated. After you cross Lake Street along an ele-

HOW TO GET THERE

From Chicago, take I–94 west to Golf Road, then go west on Golf Road to the Chick Evans Golf Course. Turn left into the parking lot.

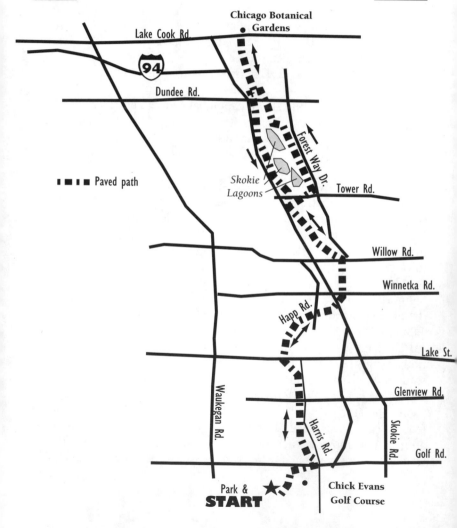

Chicago Botanical Gardens

Lake Cook Rd.

94

Dundee Rd.

Forest Way Dr.

Skokie Lagoons

Tower Rd.

■ ■ ■ Paved path

Willow Rd.

Winnetka Rd.

Happ Rd.

Lake St.

Glenview Rd.

Waukegan Rd.

Harris Rd.

Skokie Rd.

Golf Rd.

Park & **START**

Chick Evans Golf Course

DIRECTIONS

FOR

THE RIDE

0.0 Turn right onto trail from parking lot
   and head north.
1.2 Cross Glenview Road.
2.1 Cross Lake Street overpass.
3.9 Cross Winnetka Road.
4.5 Cross Willow Road.
6.1 Turn right at fork.
6.5 Cross Tower Road.
6.9 Pass beneath I–94 underpass.
8.4 Cross Dundee Road. Turn around at Chicago Botanical
   Gardens.
10.3 Pass Tower Road.
14.7 Cross Lake Street overpass.
16.8 Return to parking lot.

vated bike overpass, then bike through a tunnel underpass beneath I–94, you'll discover that the river that has snaked along the eastern portion of trail gets wider. Soft sounds and a fleeting glimpse of the highway infringing on your journey mean the lagoons are ahead.

The Skokie Lagoons are a series of lakelike waterways built by the Civilian Conservation Corps during the Great Depression. Many have small islands which prevent a clear view to the opposite side. Fishing and boating bring a fair share of small boats to the lagoons, and in-line skaters often choose this loop during the summer months. This is a good opportunity to bring your pace down a notch and be on the lookout. After you ride along the eastern loop with open fields to the east, passing Lake Cook Road indicates that the gardens are ahead.

Though it's possible to ride through the botanical gardens, it's almost better to lock your bike at the main building, bring your water bottle, and walk along at a pace at which you can appreciate this suburban treasure. If you do choose to bike in the gardens, the pace is a tad slower, and the trail gets a bit narrower. With a rose garden, a Japanese garden, an English garden, a fruit and vegetable garden, and a waterfall garden, stopping to smell the flowers has never been so easy. The 385 acres have twenty different sections to enjoy.

21

Southern Section of Robert McClory Bike Path (Green Bay Trail)

Number of miles:	26.8
Approximate pedaling time:	5½ hours
Terrain:	Flat, mostly limestone
Traffic:	Light
Things to see:	Ravinia
Food and facilities:	Many restaurants in towns along trail; public rest rooms at train stations

In July 1997 the Green Bay Trail and the North Shore Trail were collectively renamed the Robert McClory Bike Path to honor a government official who is said to have loved a good bike ride along this trail. Though new signs have been put up trailside, people still seem to call it the Green Bay Trail—to distinguish it from the North Shore Trail, which forks to the west and north beyond Rockland Road. Whatever it's called, this is probably the most often-ridden rails-to-trails conversion in the state.

The trail runs flat and next to the Metra North line from Kenilworth to Winnetka, then on to Glencoe, Highland Park, Highwood, and Lake Forest. It allows you to cover some serious ground while stopping in some charming towns along the way. This is a ride on which to bring a little extra money, for a great lunch and a little shopping along the way. As you ride along the railroad, you're between Green Bay and Sheridan Roads. Not far east of Sheridan Road lies Lake Michigan, which should give you an idea why these towns are so pleasing and the houses so nice: This is prime North Shore real estate.

The trail is on-again, off-again pavement; between are limestone surfaces. It does run through railroad parking lots and along

Rockland Rd.

Deerpath Ave.

Skokie Rd.

Green Bay Rd.

Old Elm Rd.

Waukegan Rd.

Prairie Ave.

Sheridan Rd.

Deerfield Rd.

Ravinia

Lake Cook Rd.

Dundee Rd.

Willow Rd.

● ● ● ● ● ● Unpaved path
⊦⊦⊦⊦⊦⊦⊦⊦⊦ Railroad tracks

Green Bay Rd.

★ Park &
START

94

HOW TO GET THERE

From Chicago, take I–94 west to Willow Road, then head east on Willow Road to Sheridan Road. Park on side streets or at the train station.

DIRECTIONS
FOR
THE RIDE

0.0 Find the trail west of Sheridan Road.
2.8 Cross Dundee Road.
3.1 Pass Lake Cook Road.
3.3 Pass Ravinia Festival parking lot.
4.9 Pass Deerfield Road.
10.3 Pass Deerpath Avenue.
12.4 Turn around at Rockland Road.
18.0 Pass Prairie Avenue.
22.4 Pass Lake Cook Road.
26.8 Return to Willow Road.

a few sidewalks, but for most of the ride, you're on trail. For the most part the trail stays east of the railroad, but you'll have to cross over for a spell at Old Elm Road. Be especially careful when crossing Dundee and Lake Cook Roads.

One great feature of this trail is the opportunity to bike to the Chicago entertainment outlet known as Ravinia. This is a large outdoor concert hall with a bandstand and grass lawn. With over eighty performances each year and lawn seating that never sells out, Ravinia is a Chicago mainstay for jazz, pop, classical, and chamber music. Folks of all ages come with picnic baskets and blankets to lay beneath the stars and listen. Along the trail, just north of Lake Cook Road, a parking entrance brings you in to a spot where you can lock your bike.

When passing Lake Cook Road, note that little more than a mile west are the Chicago Botanical Gardens and the terminus of the Skokie Trail. With but a short portage you can connect up with the Skokie Trail here (see ride 20) or, instead of turning around at Rockland Road, you can continue farther along the North Shore Path (the northern portion of the Robert McClory Bike Path).

Great Western Trail

There is a Great Western Trail that stretches from Canada to Mexico through Idaho, Utah, and Arizona, but it doesn't go through Illinois. The Great Western Trail that you can ride on in Illinois only touches two counties. What perhaps gives this trail its greatness is its uncharted character, similar to that of western territories. Or maybe it's great just because it heads west. With this in mind, take heed that the hook that draws you into Illinois's Great Western Trail is that no one else is hooked.

Shooting west just outside St. Charles, the Great Western Trail is probably one of the least-popular trails this close to Chicago, possibly because few people know about it. It's a ride on which you can truly be alone with your thoughts. Aside from bridge crossings and a few twists and turns, this is a flat, straight, semirural trail with a few streams and ponds along the way. Farm country takes over as you ride westward.

Converted from an abandoned railway that ran from St. Charles to the county line, the trail starts at the Leroy Oakes Forest Preserve, through which runs babbling Ferson Creek. The trail is paved and wooded at the start but not for long once you leave the

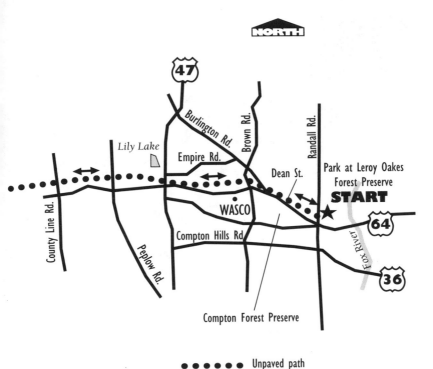

NORTH

47

Burlington Rd.

Brown Rd.

Randall Rd.

Lily Lake

Empire Rd.

Dean St.

Park at Leroy Oakes
Forest Preserve
START

County Line Rd.

WASCO

Peplow Rd.

Compton Hills Rd.

Fox River

64

36

Compton Forest Preserve

●●●●●● Unpaved path

HOW TO GET THERE From Chicago, take I–290 west to St. Charles Road, then head west on St. Charles Road to Vila Avenue. Turn left on Villa Avenue; when you reach Central Boulevard, take a right. Turn right again into the parking lot.

DIRECTIONS

FOR

THE RIDE

0.0 Start at Leroy Oakes Forest Preserve.

2.8 Cross Burlington Road.

3.0 Pass town of Wasco.

3.7 Pass Compton Lakes Forest Preserve.

5.6 Cross Brown Road.

8.2 Cross Route 47.

12.3 Turn around at Peplow Road.

24.6 Return to Leroy Oakes Forest Preserve.

preserve. Not more than a few miles east is the Fox River Trail, which runs through St. Charles. Plans for a trail connector are well under way.

What's nice about this and other such rails-to-trails efforts is that they often have bridges. Bridges are great for those of us who'd rather get our cheap thrills by going over a great arched bridge than by plummeting down a rocky, root-ridden vertical slope with fists clenched around brake levers (for that, there's Wisconsin). The bridge over Burlington Road ain't so bad in this regard.

If you run into any horseback riders on the trail, it will probably be on this part of the Great Western between Lily Lake and Leroy Oakes. After the town of Wasco, you'll pass the Campton Forest Preserve, which has a trail that goes back to the Leroy Oakes Forest Preserve and is used mostly by horseback riders.

The more scenic portions of trail are near St. Charles; the trail ends in the town of Sycamore, far past terrain it's presently worth seeing. Still, along Main Street in Sycamore, you'll find a collection of Victorian architecture in such pristine condition that it was designated a historic district in the 1970s. It has twenty-six buildings on the National Register of Historic Places. This is perhaps a better place to check out by car before you call it a day.

Fox River South

Number of miles:	23.1
Approximate pedaling time:	6½ hours
Terrain:	Flat, some hills, partly paved
Traffic:	Light
Things to see:	Windmill, Japanese gardens, nature center
Food and facilities:	Towns along the trail; rest rooms at nature center and forest preserves along the route

The southern section of the Fox River Trail is a popular haven for Illinois locals and Chicago cityfolk. More popular than the northern section due to attractions like windmills, Japanese gardens, and the many trails it links up to, the southern section of Fox River tends to draw crowds.

To start heading south along the Fox River Trail you have to cross the great bridge visible from the parking lot. There's something called the River Bend Bike Path on the river's western side, but that only goes about 3.5 miles. The bridge is fun—it's so long that it's actually two bridges separated by an island. As you reach the end, the trail hugs a huge weeping willow and proceeds through the woods. A good incline brings you up to a scenic overlook of the trail.

You're high up on the banks of the Fox River where, quite possibly, you'll enjoy the best view of the day near the Tekakwitha Woods Nature Center. This sixty-five-acre preserve has trails and an interpretive center.

HOW TO GET THERE From Chicago, take I–290 west to I–88, then I–88 west to Route 31. Go north on Route 31. Turn right into Blackhawk Forest Preserve parking lot.

31

20

25

NORTH

Blackhawk Forest Preserve
Park &
START

■ ■ ■ Paved Path

Tekakwitha Woods Nature Center

Fox River Bluff

64

Geneva Branch - Prairie P

38

Fabyan Park

Fabyan Pkwy.

31 **25**

Glenwood Park

56

88

Fox River

0.0 Turn left out of the parking lot.
0.5 Cross a bridge over the Fox River.
0.8 Pass Tekakwitha Woods Nature Center.
1.9 Pass Fox River Bluff.
7.2 Pass Geneva Branch of Prairie Path.
9.0 Pass Fabyan Forest Preserve.
11.5 Turn around at Glenwood Park.
23.1 Return to parking lot.

A little farther along—right after a decline that takes you into the woods—is the Fox River Bluff Forest Preserve. You'll next pass through Norris Woods and ascend out of the woods and onto the streets of St. Charles. There are a few hills even in town. Once you reach East Illinois Avenue you're back on the trail proper.

After you pass a trail connector from the Illinois Prairie Path (Geneva Branch), more fun things to see lie ahead: Fabyan Forest Preserve, the Villa Museum, the Japanese garden, and the windmill. The Fabyan resides on both sides of the Fox River; it's the former estate of Colonel George and Nelle Fabyan. Their villa is now the Villa Museum, where their collection of Oriental artifacts is on display. A recently renovated Japanese garden makes a good place to stop for a picnic. Built by two German craftsmen in the 1850s, a 68-foot windmill affords the preserve a refreshing novelty. The windmill, moved in 1914 by Colonel Fabyan to its present spot, was featured on a 1979 postage stamp and was used by the estate to mill flour for bread during World War I.

Coming out of Glenwood Park, notice the gentle rapid formed by a broken dam on the Fox River. This is about as rough as things get in this portion of the river.

Northern Section of Robert McClory Bike Path (North Shore Path)

Number of miles:	29.5
Approximate pedaling time:	6 hours
Terrain:	Flat, mostly unpaved
Traffic:	Moderate
Things to see:	Naval Training Center
Food and facilities:	Few places along the trail; rest rooms at train station in Lake Bluff

If you ride the northern portion of the Robert McClory Bike Path, better known as the North Shore Path, you'll have the opportunity to tell people you biked to Wisconsin and back. The best of this path is the beginning portion, before you reach North Chicago and Waukegan.

The drive up to the North Shore Trail from Chicago can be a good study in North Shore architecture if you take the more scenic route along Sheridan. It's best to stay out of the left lane so that you don't get held up at intersections by cars trying to make left turns. Watch for signs that keep you on Sheridan Road (there are some turns along Sheridan, but they are well marked).

If you park at the train station and notice the street that wraps around a small collection of stores, you'll realize that even the commercial section of Lake Bluff is quite beautiful. The North Shore Path heads west and north at Rockland Road, picking up where the Green Bay Trail (see ride 21) leaves off. The actual split occurs south of Rockland Road. Though the western branch is worth exploring, the idea of making it to Wisconsin on bike is, for people like me, too enticing to pass up.

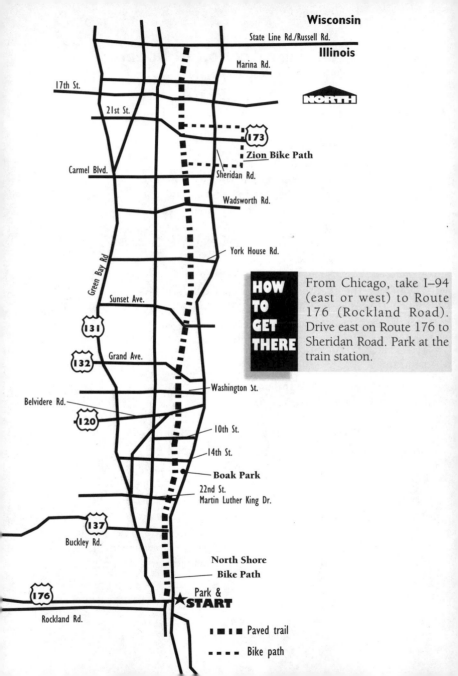

Wisconsin

State Line Rd./Russell Rd.

Illinois

Marina Rd.

17th St.

21st St.

173

Zion Bike Path

Carmel Blvd.

Sheridan Rd.

Wadsworth Rd.

York House Rd.

Green Bay Rd.

Sunset Ave.

131

132

Grand Ave.

Washington St.

Belvidere Rd.

120

10th St.

14th St.

Boak Park

22nd St.
Martin Luther King Dr.

137

Buckley Rd.

North Shore
Bike Path

176

Rockland Rd.

Park &
★**START**

NORTH

HOW TO GET THERE From Chicago, take I–94 (east or west) to Route 176 (Rockland Road). Drive east on Route 176 to Sheridan Road. Park at the train station.

▬ ▬ ▬ Paved trail

- - - - Bike path

DIRECTIONS
FOR
THE RIDE

0.0 Turn left out of parking lot.
2.6 Pass Route 137.
2.9 Pass Martin Luther King Drive.
5.0 Pass Belvidere Road.
7.4 Pass Sunset Avenue.
9.0 Pass York House Road.
9.8 Turn right at Carmel Boulevard to access Zion Bike Path.
13.6 Return to North Shore Path.
15.6 Turn around at Wisconsin state line.
18.0 Pass 21st Street.
23.5 Pass Route 132.
29.5 Return to parking lot.

The trail starts out right next to Sheridan Road; it's as if the trail is just another straight road running alongside Sheridan for a bit. Once you're past 22nd Street, you'll be entering North Chicago—but not before you pass the Great Lakes Naval Training Station on your right. Its average command population was forty-eight thousand in 1997. This includes recruits, students, military and civilian staff, and dependents. It's the largest naval training center in the navy, the largest military installation in the state of Illinois, and the third largest naval base in the navy. It's about sixteen hundred acres in all. Only portions are visible from the trail.

Once you hit 22nd Street, cross the tracks and pick up the trail at Boak Park. The path here departs from Sheridan Road on its way through North Chicago and Waukegan, both well-developed areas with a lot of streets to cross (the least-attractive part of the ride).

Once you pass Russell Road you've reached the border. Soon after, the Kenosha County Trail continues. For a pleasant distraction, check out the Zion Park District loop you'll pass at 17th Street. A bit farther east the Illinois Beach State Park runs along the coast through Winthrop Harbor and Zion.

 **Palos**

Number of miles:	11
Approximate pedaling time:	3½ hours
Terrain:	Very hilly, unpaved
Traffic:	None
Things to see:	Little Red Schoolhouse
Food and facilities:	Little nearby; rest rooms throughout preserve

Ask anyone. The best mountain biking in Cook County is at Palos. It's so good and so popular, in fact, that some of the single track has been closed to mountain bikers. Though you can still enjoy some of what once was, when the word *Palos* is used among mountain bikers these days, it's often out of regret. Trail openings and closings change frequently depending on weather conditions and restoration progress, so be on the lookout. The trails are patrolled and tickets are given out if you are found on a trail you're not supposed to be on. Within the forest preserve, certain areas are designated nature preserves; these are more likely to be closed off. Portions south of 95th Street as well as toward the end of this ride may be in question. Also be on the lookout for four kinds of signs: The gray confidence marker guides you through the trail; the orange trail-closure marker tells you to keep out; the special-restriction sign tells you a trail is in danger of being closed; and the triangular bird sign reminds you to stay on the trail through a preserved area.

From Chicago, you can get to Palos inside 45 minutes. It's pretty easy, though crossing the canals may throw you off. You should go over two waterways on Willow Springs Road; if you

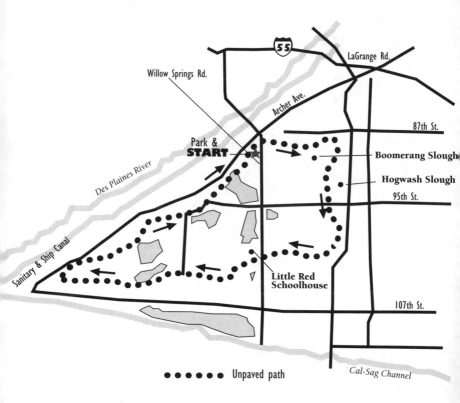

NORTH

Willow Springs Rd.

55

LaGrange Rd.

Archer Ave.

87th St.

Park & **START**

Boomerang Slough

Des Plaines River

Hogwash Slough

95th St.

Sanitary & Ship Canal

Little Red Schoolhouse

107th St.

●●●●● Unpaved path

Cal-Sag Channel

HOW TO GET THERE From Chicago, take I–55 west to Willow Springs Road. Go south on Willow Springs Road past Archer Avenue. Turn left into the parking area.

DIRECTIONS

FOR
THE RIDE

0.0 Turn right onto trail.
1.4 Pass trail intersection.
2.7 Turn left.
3.7 Pass Willow Springs Road.
3.8 Turn right at fork.
5.2 Pass through parking lot to pick up trail
     on other side.
5.8 Go straight through trail intersection.
6.4 Go straight through intersection.
7.7 Turn left at fork.
9.1 Turn left at fork.
11.0 Return to parking lot.

pass three you've gone too far. Once you're inside the preserve, little connects you to what's outside. There aren't trail bridges over or under streets; you just cross and pick up where you left off.

The start of the ride is pretty mild. As you ride out of Boomerang Slough into Hogwash Slough heading north, you'll find the trail to be in good condition. Though Palos is great for hills, it's not so great on trail markings. It's easy to get lost. Bring a compass if you can. Remember that you started in the northeastern part of the preserve.

As you cross Willow Springs Road, you'll see the Little Red Schoolhouse on your right. Now the center of many forest preserve activities, way back when it acted as a one-room schoolhouse for farm kids, who commuted from miles around. In the 1950s it was converted to a nature center. Exhibits inside and out educate on the natural surroundings. These exhibits include snake presentations, insect tutorials, and a collection of farm equipment. Past the Little Red Schoolhouse, things get more challenging along the single tracks—though these areas are not always open. Enjoying the hills at Palos is still possible, but it takes patience and understanding.

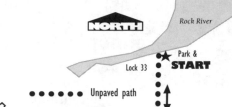

HOW TO GET THERE

From Chicago, take I–55 west to I–80, then I–80 west to Route 40. Turn north on Route 40. Turn right into the parking area.

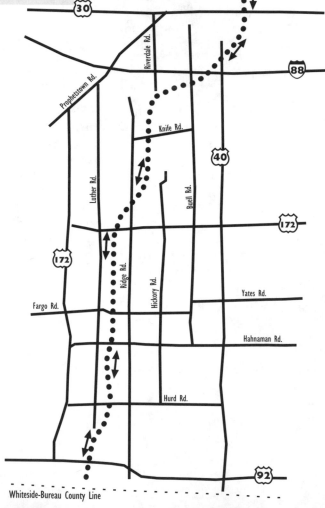

NORTH

Rock River

Lock 33

Park & START

•••••• Unpaved path

30

Riverdale Rd.

88

Prophetstown Rd.

Knife Rd.

40

Luther Rd.

Buell Rd.

172

172

Ridge Rd.

Hickory Rd.

Yates Rd.

Fargo Rd.

Hahnaman Rd.

Hurd Rd.

92

Whiteside-Bureau County Line

Hennepin Canal Feeder Trail

Number of miles:	31.4
Approximate pedaling time:	6½ hours
Terrain:	Flat, unpaved
Traffic:	None
Things to see:	Canal locks
Food and facilities:	Rest rooms in Rock Falls

The drive out to the Hennepin Canal Trail is a journey to the center of the state, into a rural area of Illinois where there are off-trail concessions only. It's hard to say which is straighter, a canal towpath or a rails-to-trail conversion. The presence of the canal makes the former *seem* more open, though. It's almost as if you can see for miles.

The Hennepin Canal scenario is a common one. It's a man-made channel built with the intention of creating a commercial shipping route from the Illinois River to the Mississippi River (as was the plan with the I & M Canal; see ride 19). Yet by the time the Hennepin Feeder Canal had been completed, trains were able to transport goods more quickly. Thus, the Hennepin became a dinosaur before its time. However, it's interesting to note that for bikers, hikers, and cross-country skiers, this historical succession of shipping methodology—from canal to train to plane—has left behind quite a few great trails, the Hennepin included. What's nice about this canal trail is that there are no surprises. You know what you are getting into and you know who's on the trail with you.

The canal is 104.5 miles long and 5,773 acres in all. Its inverted **T** shape runs west to the Mississippi at Rock Island, east to

DIRECTIONS

FOR

THE RIDE

0.0 Start at Rock Falls parking area.
3.1 Pass I-88.
5.0 Pass Knife Road.
9.8 Pass Route 172.
12.0 Pass Fargo Road.
15.7 Turn around at Whiteside-Bureau County line.
31.4 Return to parking lot.

the Illinois River in Bureau, and north to Lake Sinnissippi at Rock Falls. For many years there was a large grain elevator at Mile Nine; farmers brought their grain here for shipping before the days of railroad. At one point blocks of ice were cut from the canal and sold in the winter months.

At the start of the trail in Rock Falls, check out one of thirty-two locks that are part of the canal. Though never used for its original purpose, this mostly limestone path was once what's called a towpath—intended to be walked by animals towing the water vessels. The trail is almost all flat and a pleasant ride; it's shielded by a high bank on each side of the canal. As you ride past many roads, you're not impeded: You ride beneath them under some ten bridges.

For a breather and some info on how locks work, stop in at the visitors center in Sheffield. There's also a brief history of the canal's past. An interesting aspect of some locks along the canal is the Marshall gate, which opens outward, much like a rural roadside mailbox.

Indian Boundary Trail

Number of miles:	10.6
Approximate pedaling time:	3 hours
Terrain:	Dirt, some hills, unpaved
Traffic:	Light
Things to see:	Forest, railroad tracks
Food and facilities:	None near trail; rest rooms at Trailside Museum and at trail turnoffs

The Indian Boundary gets its name from a boundary line that spanned from Lake Michigan to Ottawa; it served as a territorial boundary between the Potawatomi tribe and European settlers in 1816.

The Indian Boundary is directly west of Chicago, so that you'll encouter many of the major east–west Chicago street names as you ride along the Des Plaines River. Getting here is easy, though: All you do is drive straight west from the north side of Chicago. A good place to park and hit the trail is the Trailside Museum, which offers ample parking facilities across the street from the trail. You'll find access to the trail by riding along an interior road across the way, then bearing left along the edges of great playing fields surrounded by trees and shrubs. The trail is at the tree line in the corner of the field.

This path is an offshoot from the main trail along the river. In the summer vegetation closes you off completely from the preserves and the surrounding streets.

CAUTION: The Indian Boundary Trail is great because it seems authentically made by feet and tire treads, but it is highly unregulated. I've never seen a police officer on it. Dogs are often

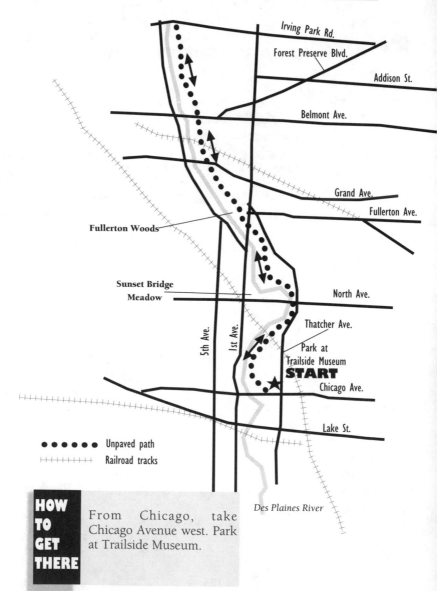

Irving Park Rd.

Forest Preserve Blvd.

Addison St.

Belmont Ave.

Grand Ave.

Fullerton Ave.

Fullerton Woods

**Sunset Bridge
Meadow**

North Ave.

Thatcher Ave.

Park at
Trailside Museum
START

Chicago Ave.

5th Ave.

Ist Ave.

Lake St.

●●●●● Unpaved path

┼┼┼┼┼┼ Railroad tracks

Des Plaines River

**HOW
TO
GET
THERE** From Chicago, take
Chicago Avenue west. Park
at Trailside Museum.

DIRECTIONS
FOR
THE RIDE

0.0 Find trail along Des Plaines River.
1.0 Cross railroad tracks.
1.7 Cross North Avenue.
3.2 Cross Grand Avenue.
4.3 Cross Belmont Avenue.
5.3 Turn around at Irving Park Road.
10.6 Return to parking lot.

off their leashes. The trail is primitive. There are lots of mosquitoes. Another thing to keep in mind is ground conditions. Rainfall makes Indian Boundary a mud bath. Fat tires are a requirement. If these thing don't bother you, the joy of the trail is yours.

The railroad tracks you come to can, at times, be crossed close to the riverbanks; other times going up and over them is the drier choice. The bridge would seem a perfect high school delinquent hangout, indeed, the presence of outwardly expressive youth is verified by the graffiti high up on the bridge.

As you ride along this very flat trail, you'll at times have to cross busy streets—which in fact may help you keep your bearings. At Thatcher Avenue, carrying your bike over a guardrail or two is necessary, but you're back into the woods in a flash. Railroad crossings, as noted, require a little extra effort. Many portions of the trail are flat, but there are places where mountain bikers have ripped through a ravine, causing a lot of erosion. Cross to the west bank at the North Avenue bridge. As you continue northward two more railroad track crossings arise before Belmont. If you venture farther along the Indian Boundary, you'll go right under the northwest tollway, where a familiar airline billboard with a digital clock is visible to those on their way to O'Hare Airport. The trail stays out of sight, unnoticeable to those on the expressway.

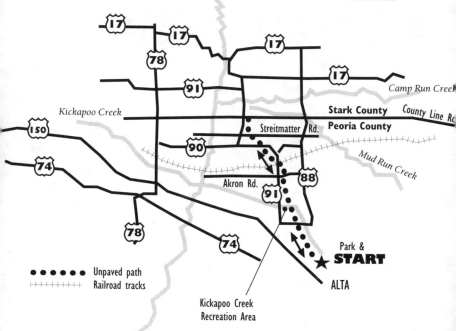

Spoon River

Camp Run Creek

Stark County   County Line Rd
Peoria County

Kickapoo Creek

Streitmatter Rd.

Mud Run Creek

Akron Rd.

Park &
START

ALTA

•••••• Unpaved path
++++++++ Railroad tracks

Kickapoo Creek
Recreation Area

HOW TO GET THERE

From Chicago, take I–55 west to I–74. Drive west on I–74 to I–474. Take Route 474 east to Route 6. Turn north on Route 6, then left into the parking lot.

Rock Island State Trail

Number of miles:	19
Approximate pedaling time:	3½ hours
Terrain:	Flat, unpaved
Traffic:	None
Things to see:	Culvert, bridges
Food and facilities:	Few places to stop; rest rooms at Kickapoo Creek Recreational Area

The drive out to the Rock Island State Trail is farm, farm, and—you guessed it—more farm. Rows and rows of corn grew as high as my jeep as I raced westward. With the top down and the sun quickly falling, I made it to the town of Alta quicker than I would have guessed on country roads with dirt driveway turnoffs. Alta, population one hundred, used to be the trailhead for the Rock Island State Trail until they extended it on down to Peoria in 1995.

As you ride north out of Alta, on your left are fourteen acres of restored prairie, part of the Kickapoo Creek Recreational Area; camping facilities include pit toilets, fire pads, picnic tables, and water. Farther past Alta, mature trees form a natural canopy from the hot rays of the midwestern sun just before you pass through an arched culvert.

This is a ride for taking it easy. In farm country things need not move fast to be satisfying. Continuing clear on into the next county, the trail ain't goin' anywhere (except it closes at sundown). It runs over 30 miles one-way all the way into Toulon. Too much for one day.

The Rock Island State Trail—long and flat as it is—was once a

DIRECTIONS
FOR
THE RIDE

0.0 Start at old trailhead in Alta.
0.3 Cross Kickapoo Creek.
3.9 Cross Akron Road.
6.1 Cross railroad tracks.
6.4 Cross Route 90.
7.3 Cross Streitmatter Road.
9.5 Turn around at County Line Road.
19.0 Return to parking lot.

railroad line that ran for the first time in 1871 from nearby Peoria to Rock Island over on Illinois's border with Iowa. It ran for forty years until no one used it anymore. Peoria's Forest Park Foundation acquired the abandoned railway corridor in June 1965 and deeded the property to the Department of Conservation four years later.

The trail is mostly dirt and limestone, as a farm trail would be. After you pass over the railroad tracks and through the slightly larger town of Princeville, you'll come upon what's called a prairie remnant. This is a mesic prairie—a moderately moist environment. Big bluestem, Indian grass, northern dropseed, and blue joint grasses grow wild along this stretch, which crosses over into Stark County. The trail crosses over Mud Run Creek, Camp Run Creek, and Spoon River via a great trestle.

During the summer of 1998, the Rock Island State Trail became an interplanetary bike ride. Billed as the world's largest model of the solar system (and in the *Guinness Book of World Records)*, the trail allowed you to travel anywhere from 10 to 45 miles to reach places like Jupiter and Saturn. You could get to Pluto by biking 100 miles, with the option of seeing some of the moons as well.

Tinley Creek

Number of miles:	16.4
Approximate pedaling time:	1½ hours
Terrain:	Hilly, paved
Traffic:	None
Things to see:	Prairie
Facilities:	Rest rooms near parking lots or the preserve

Tinley Creek is a well-maintained, established forest preserve no more than half an hour southwest of Chicago. It's one of eight designated bike trails in the forest preserve district of Chicago's Cook County. There's plenty of parking and facilities. The preserve has something for both pavement pounders and fat-tire fiends.

Its hills are essentially made up of glacial drift left behind from the last ice age. As the glacier receded, topographic ripples collectively formed a ridge now covered with wood and prairie. Geologists call this area Tinley Moraine.

This ride does anything but stay true to the path of Tinley Creek. It's a path built for speed, with smooth pavement and nothing to slow you down except a few street crossings. Open flat prairie, partially cleared woods, and forest areas stretch through Tinley.

You'll ride away from Arrowhead Lake with open parkland and roadside views. The trail remains very flat at its start, but remember to slow down before crossing 135th Street: This street is busy near rush hour and on weekends.

After you pass 135th Street, Turtlehead Lake comes into view, a body of water created not by a glacier but by the need for earth fill

131st St.

Arrowhead Lake

135th St.

Park & **START**

Tinley Creek

NORTH

Turtlehead Lake

P

P

P

P

Midlothian Tpke.

143rd St.

82nd Ave.

147th St.

151st St.

Central Ave.

Cicero Ave.

Crawford Ave.

159th St.

Golf Course

Harlem Ave.

Oak Park Ave.

167th St.

57

175th St.

80

80

57

■ ■ ■ ■ Paved trail

P Parking lot

++++++++ Railroad tracks

HOW TO GET THERE

From Chicago, take I–55 west to Route 43 (Harlem Avenue). Drive south on Route 43 until you reach 135th Street, where you turn left. Then turn left again into the parking lot.

DIRECTIONS
FOR
THE RIDE

0.0 Turn left onto trail from the parking lot of Arrowhead Lake.

0.2 Pass Harlem Avenue.

3.1 Pass intersection of 143rd Street and Harlem Avenue.

4.9 Turn left at fork.

5.5 Cross intersection of 151st Street and Oak Park Avenue.

6.1 Cross 159th Street. Turn right at fork.

9.2 Cross 159th Street again.

10.8 Cross 151st Street.

16.4 Return to parking lot.

along the Tri-State Expressway. Though no longer parklike, hedges, wildflowers, and prairie grass bank the trail.

After a huge bridge clearing Tinley Creek, past one of two trail tunnels, you'll find intersections with single-track trail offshoots that run right through the creek and over rocky areas. Those in need of some off-road mayhem can check out here for a while. These trails will bring you west of Harlem Avenue any-which-way through an unplanned web of trail links.

At 159th Street you can view the Chicago skyline on a clear day right off the trail. The asphalt twists and turns through flat prairie fields, then runs up and down through the Yankee Woods area while looping around the George W. Dunne Golf Course.

The Tinley Creek Preserve extends much farther north-south than it does east-west. There are southern trails, but they're at the other end of the preserve, south of I–80. Though there's been talk of trail improvements in recent years, there seems to be little action involved yet. The idea is to link the northern trails to the southern for a total of 33 trail miles. We'll see if it actually happens.

30 Prairie Avenue Historic South Loop

Number of miles:	6.6
Approximate pedaling time:	1½ hours
Terrain:	Flat, paved
Traffic:	Heavy on weekdays
Things to see:	Architecture
Food and facilities:	Many places to stop; rest rooms at the Vietnam Veterans Museum

The Prairie District is one of the lesser-known Chicago sights. It's south of Grant Park and west of Soldier Field on the other side of the train tracks. It's that place you can see from Lake Shore Drive near all the new condo development that seems to be taking over Chicago. This ride pieces together a part of Chicago that once was the crème de la crème.

Though Grant Park is well used for events like Jazz-fest, Taste of Chicago, and the Chicago Marathon, it's underutilized on off weekends—which makes it the perfect place to ride through most of the time. Naturally, Buckingham Fountain brings in its share of tourists, who spill over from the lakefront, Navy Pier, and Museum Campus, but the sculptures and first-rate gardens of Grant Park make for a great slow meander, anyway. It's a nice prelude to the Prairie District and the south loop.

Once you're through Grant Park and on Indiana Avenue, you're venturing into an area where fewer people go. You're south of the Michigan Avenue attractions and approaching a trestle. The pavement is smooth and flat and fewer cars are on the streets. A huge cluster of condominium town homes is on your left.

As you turn onto 18th Street, the fun starts. A small cafe that's part of the Vietnam Veterans Museum and keeps unreliable hours marks the beginning of the Prairie Avenue Historic District. These few blocks used to be the richest in Chicago. It all changed by 1900 when the Palmer family, one of the most powerful in Chicago, moved north to the Gold Coast, buying up a good portion of it to later sell off at over four times the price they'd paid. These days, while some Prairie District buildings are occupied by businesses or organizations, many of the beautiful homes have been torn down. Plaques along the streets tell the stories of this area and its architecture. This is another good place to go slow and enjoy.

Your next stop is an area known as Printer's Row, once a center for printing in Chicago; it's now a largely residential area of high-rises just south of the Loop. Traffic is less of a problem until you hit Congress Parkway. After you reach Wacker Drive you will be taken north, then east through downtown and along the Chicago River, an area that's extremely busy during the week but much less so over the weekend. Among many other Chicago mainstays, you'll pass the Sears Tower.

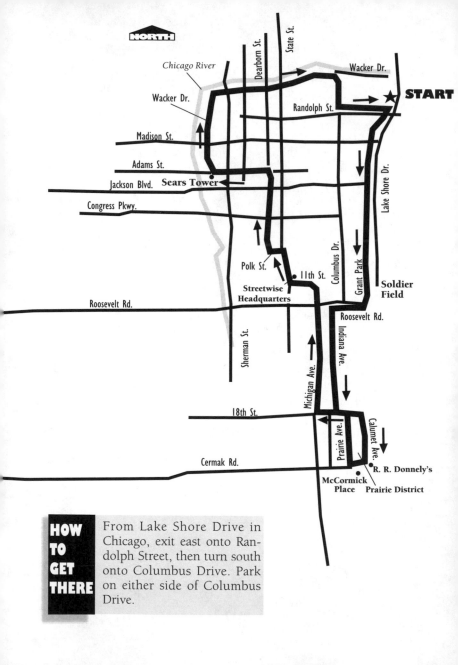

NORTH

Chicago River

Wacker Dr.

Wacker Dr.

Dearborn St.

State St.

Randolph St.

START

Madison St.

Lake Shore Dr.

Adams St.

Jackson Blvd. **Sears Tower**

Congress Pkwy.

Columbus Dr.

Grant Park

Polk St.

• 11th St.

Streetwise Headquarters

Soldier Field

Roosevelt Rd.

Roosevelt Rd.

Sherman St.

Michigan Ave.

Indiana Ave.

18th St.

Prairie Ave.

Calumet Ave.

Cermak Rd.

• R. R. Donnely's

McCormick Place   **Prairie District**

HOW TO GET THERE From Lake Shore Drive in Chicago, exit east onto Randolph Street, then turn south onto Columbus Drive. Park on either side of Columbus Drive.

DIRECTIONS
FOR
THE RIDE

0.0 Enter eastern side of Grant Park at Randolph Street.

1.1 Take second right past Museum Campus entrance.

1.2 Turn right onto Roosevelt Road.

1.3 Turn left onto Indiana Avenue.

2.1 Turn left onto 18th Street. Pass Vietnam Veterans Museum.

2.5 Turn right onto Calumet Avenue.

2.7 Pass R. R. Donnely's Lakeside Press.

2.8 Turn right onto Cermak Road before McCormick Place entrance.

2.9 Turn right onto Prairie Avenue.

3.2 Turn left onto 18th Street again.

3.4 Turn right onto Michigan Avenue. Turn left onto 11th Street.

3.9 Pass Streetwise Headquarters.

4.4 Turn right onto State Street.

4.6 Turn left onto Polk Street.

4.7 Turn right onto Dearborn Street.

5.2 Turn left onto Adams Street.

5.4 Turn right onto Wacker Drive.

6.2 Turn right onto Columbus Drive.

6.4 Turn left onto Randolph Street.

6.5 Turn right through park.

6.6 Return to start of the ride.

River North

Number of miles:	5.2
Approximate pedaling time:	1½ hours
Terrain:	Flat, paved
Traffic:	Heavy on weekdays
Things to see:	Architecture, art galleries
Food and facilities:	North Pier and restaurants chains along the route; no public rest rooms

This is a ride for Chicago newcomers who need a quick tour of what's just on the edge of the Loop. It's also for art lovers and shoppers, because everything about this area is chic—it's the luxury and fashion alternative to the straitlaced Loop. It includes Michigan Avenue and the art galleries to the west. This ride starts out in the luxurious Gold Coast and slowly works its way into Streeterville, which is closer to the city but hardly a desirable place to live. It lacks anything authentic. It's touristy.

Oak Street is known far and wide as *the* street to shop on. It's filled with big-name boutiques and clothiers like Armani and Versace. This street is crowded all the time; be on the lookout for maniacal parking attendants.

After you cross Michigan Avenue, the lake comes into view as you ride along Inner Lake Shore Drive. In-line skaters often brave this sidewalk despite traffic turning off the drive.

As you head south after passing the Museum of Contemporary Art and Northwestern Hospital, you'll come to River North, sort of an extension of Navy Pier's carnivalesque atmosphere. Inside North Pier are food and shops selling everything from kites to candy.

NORTH

Esquire Theater

Park & **START**

Oak St.

Oak St.

Inner Lake Shore Drive

Division St.

Chicago Ave.

Michigan Ave.

Fairbanks Ct.

Franklin St.

Newberry Library

Hard Rock Cafe

W. Ontario St.

Ohio St.

Illinois St.

Kinzie St.

Pizzeria Uno

State St.

Wabah Ave.

North New St.

North Pier

McClurg Ct.

East River Dr.

Melas Fountain

Chicago River

Wrigley Building

Tribune Building

La Salle St.

Dearborn St.

NBC Building

Columbus Dr.

Lake Shore Dr.

Lake Michigan

HOW TO GET THERE From Chicago's Lake Shore Drive, exit east onto North Avenue, then continue south on Inner Lake Shore Drive until you reach Cedar Street. Turn right onto Cedar Street. Park on either side of Cedar Street.

DIRECTIONS

FOR
THE RIDE

0.0 Start at corner of Oak and State Streets
   Head east on Oak Street.
0.1 Turn left onto Oak Street.
0.2 Pass Esquire Theater.
0.3 Cross Michigan Avenue.
0.4 Turn right onto Inner Lake Shore Drive.
0.9 Turn right onto Chicago Avenue.

1.0 Pass Northwestern University Law School.
1.1 Pass Museum of Contemporary Art on left.
1.2 Turn left onto Fairbanks Court.
1.5 Turn left onto Illinois Street.
1.6 Turn right onto McClurg Court before North Pier. Turn right
   onto East River Drive.
1.8 Pass Nicholas J. Melas Fountain.
1.9 Turn right onto North New Street.
2.0 Turn left onto Illinois Street.
2.1 Turn left onto Fairbanks Court.
2.2 Turn right onto North Water Street. Pass NBC Building.
2.3 Cross through paved park. Pass Tribune Building.
2.4 Cross Michigan Avenue. Pass Wrigley Building.
2.7 Pass Benito Juarez bust as you ride through paved park.
2.8 Turn right onto Wabash Avenue.
2.9 Pass Pizzeria Uno.
3.0 Turn left onto Ontario Street.
3.4 Turn right onto Franklin Street.
3.7 Turn right onto Chicago Avenue.
4.0 Turn right onto Dearborn Street.
4.4 Pass Newbery Library.
4.7 Turn right onto Oak Street.

After passing the NBC Building, you'll ride along the sidewalk between two tall buildings. As you emerge, you'll notice the famous Tribune Building on your right and the Wrigley Building in front of you. Cross Michigan Avenue carefully. It's higher than some of the other streets. Though there are steps to bring you down to a lower level, this won't be necessary. Ride over the pedestrian bridge near the health club and turn right onto Wabash. Farther up you'll pass Pizzeria Uno, the original restaurant from which the chain sprang.

Continuing north and west things get cheesy with the Rain Forest Cafe, Hard Rock Cafe, and Planet Hollywood all within a few blocks. Once you're past this cluster, you'll come upon Franklin Street, in the heart of what's considered River North. Art galleries abound on the left and right. For a look at what's going on in the Chicago art market, you couldn't ask for a better locale. There are a few good places to grab a bite in this area while you take in some art.

Uptown

Number of miles:	8
Approximate pedaling time:	2½ hours
Terrain:	Flat, paved
Traffic:	Moderate
Things to see:	Architecture, neighborhoods
Food and facilities:	Heartland Cafe

Uptown is what you'd call a vintage ride. It's one of the last great architectural neighborhoods not yet gentrified—which is probably why at Uptown's famous Green Mill, I once heard a bongo-drumming band perform a song titled, "Condominium Ad Infinitum." The architecture of Uptown is beaux arts, with very ornate stone facades. Considered the hip hangout in the Roaring Twenties, many ballrooms once filled with elegant socialites dressed to the nines now host a retro-concert-going, martini-drinking crowd.

As you start out at Wilson and Broadway, the corner El stop signifies the architectural beginning point of Uptown. The elegant stone columns—now dilapidated—tell the story of the days when this terminal brought patrons into Uptown clubs and restaurants. When older train lines began to bypass Uptown, no longer bringing travelers from different cities through this attractive neighborhood, it quickly fell into disrepair. The streets are busy in this area, so use caution as you ride north.

On your right you'll pass a great long building that gives you your first real idea of what the rest of Uptown will be like. Though many urban shops line the lower section, the rest of the facade is heavily ornamented with columns, leaded glass, and arches. Ahead is the unofficial heart of Uptown: the Green Mill, the Uptown Na-

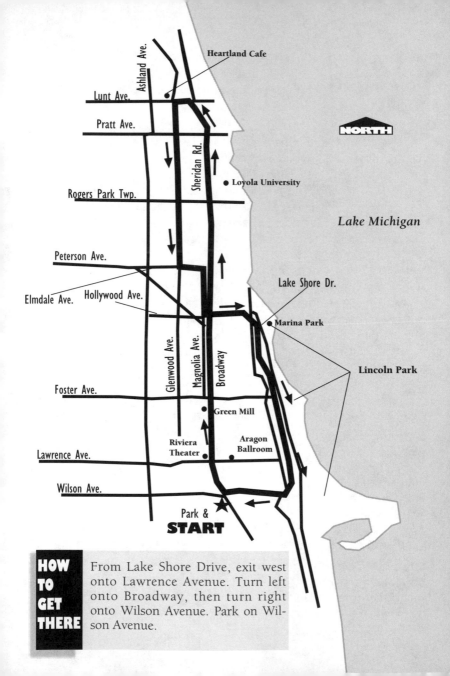

Heartland Cafe

Ashland Ave.

Lunt Ave.

Pratt Ave.

Sheridan Rd.

NORTH

Rogers Park Twp.

● Loyola University

Lake Michigan

Peterson Ave.

Elmdale Ave.   Hollywood Ave.

Lake Shore Dr.

Glenwood Ave.

Magnolia Ave.

Broadway

● Marina Park

Lincoln Park

Foster Ave.

● Green Mill

Riviera
Theater ●

Aragon
Ballroom

Lawrence Ave.

Wilson Ave.

Park &
START

**HOW
TO
GET
THERE**
From Lake Shore Drive, exit west
onto Lawrence Avenue. Turn left
onto Broadway, then turn right
onto Wilson Avenue. Park on Wilson Avenue.

DIRECTIONS

FOR

THE RIDE

0.0 Head north on Broadway from El stop at Broadway and Wilson Avenues.

0.4 Pass Riviera Theater.

0.5 Pass Green Mill.

1.3 Pass Catholic church.

2.4 Pass Loyola University.

3.1 Turn left onto Lunt Avenue.

3.4 Turn left onto Glenwood Avenue.

4.6 Turn left at Elmdale Avenue traffic circle.

5.2 Turn right onto Magnolia Avenue.

5.3 Turn left onto Hollywood Avenue.

6.7 Turn right into Marina Park.

7.4 Turn right onto Wilson Avenue.

8.0 Return to Broadway Avenue.

tional Bank, the Riviera, the Uptown Theater, and the Aragon Ballroom.

The Green Mill, a favorite hangout of Al Capone, hosts many small jazz bands and a slightly intellectual crowd. On Sundays it features an open-mike poetry slam. The Uptown Theater is in disrepair, but the Riviera and Aragon both book big-name bands that attract sizable crowds. The Aragon has gone through the most laughable of transformations. During the 1920s and 1930s it was, of course, a huge ballroom for dancing. Many big-band musicians played at the Aragon with its great domed ceiling and painted clouds overhead—ensuring that patrons' dreams came true here. These days bands like Big Head Todd and the Monsters or Ben Folds Five bring in hordes of kids of all ages in ripped jeans and goatees.

As you continue into Rogers Park, things get a bit urban until you reach the Heartland Cafe, a crunchy restaurant with great food. On your return southward, the residential neighborhoods offer relief from urban streets. While riding along the El, be especially careful at the blind intersections. The ride among the many residential bungalows is not busy, so you can enjoy these more northerly residences of Rogers Park and Uptown.

Bohemian Bucktown

Number of miles:	4.5
Approximate pedaling time:	1 hour
Terrain:	Flat, paved
Traffic:	Moderate
Things to see:	Restaurants, shops, neighborhoods
Food and facilities:	Restaurants throughout Bucktown; no public rest rooms

Bucktown might more appropriately be called X-town, due to all the Gen-X types that have made it popular. Make no mistake, however: What has really made Bucktown is its restaurants. For those of you who have not attempted a ride west of the expressway, I assure you there is no better way to get a sense of this neighborhood with its used book stores, its twentieth-century antiques, its Bohemian art galleries, and its very hip and decadent restaurants. The center of Bucktown is the intersection of North, Milwaukee, and Damen Avenues. Soul Kitchen, on the corner of Milwaukee and Damen, is a Bucktown staple for good food with a Cajun twist. On the opposite corner is a flatiron building similar to the one in Manhattan.

Ride down Milwaukee Avenue noting its restaurants, shops, and clubs all designed in the styles of the day. One looks like an old diner; another, called the Blue Note, has only a blue neon sign depicting a single note; the sign for a popular bar known as Holiday glimmers with reflective silver fringe much like an old Las Vegas casino sign. This is a main street, so be on the lookout for traffic. As you continue south, you'll have to jump onto Ashland Avenue for a moment to reach Division Street.

Bucktown Pub

NORTH

Jane's

Cortland St.

Leopard Lounge

Paulina St.

Wabasnia Ave.

Park &
START

North Ave.

LeMoyne St.

Holiday

Evergreen Ave.

Division St.

Wolcott Ave.

Ellen St.

Leavitt St.

Hoyne Ave.

Damen Ave.

Wood St.

Ashland Ave.

Milwaukee Ave.

94

90

HOW TO GET THERE From Chicago, take I–90/94 to North Avenue; exit west. Park on North Avenue east of Milwaukee Avenue.

0.0 From North Avenue, turn left onto Milwaukee Avenue.
0.2 Pass Holiday bar.
0.7 Turn right onto Ashland Avenue.
0.8 Turn right onto Division Street.
1.0 Turn right onto Wood Street.
1.1 Turn left onto Ellen Street.
1.4 Turn right onto Wolcott Avenue.
1.5 Turn left onto Wood Street.
2.1 Turn right onto Cortland Street.
2.3 Turn right onto Paulina Street before Bucktown Pub, Jane's, and Leopard Lounge.
2.7 Turn right onto Wabasnia Avenue.
3.2 Turn left onto Hoyne Avenue.
3.6 Turn right onto Lemoyne Street.
3.7 Turn left onto Leavitt Street.
3.9 Turn left onto Evergreen Avenue.
4.0 Turn left onto Hoyne Avenue.
4.3 Turn right onto North Avenue.
4.5 Return to Milwaukee Avenue.

Division Street is the divider between Wicker Park and Bucktown. The shops along Division are less known to outsiders but they won't remain so for long, given to clubs like Liquid Kitty that seem a bit too hip. Turn right onto Wood Street and you'll begin to explore some of the real-estate steals early developers bought up as Bucktown came into favor.

Farther north on Wood Street, the charm of residential Bucktown will become more apparent. As you turn onto Cortland, a few corner joints come into view. Jane's serves a mean brunch, and the Leopard Lounge is *the* place to go for a martini.

As you start to head south again, you'll see some of the residen-

tial treasures of Bucktown. While brownstones in Lincoln Park and the Gold Coast are impressive, they can't match up to some of the places down here on Hoyne. There are brownstones with huge front, back, and side yards—reminiscent of what most Chicago homes were once like. The ride through these parts is nothing short of stimulating.

HOW TO GET THERE

From Chicago, take I–90/94 to Division Street. Exit west onto Division Street and drive to Humboldt Park. Parking is available in the park.

Logan Square

Number of miles:	5.7
Approximate pedaling time:	1½ hours
Terrain:	Flat, paved
Traffic:	Light
Things to see:	Logan Square, flag sculptures, boulevards
Food and facilities:	Abril on Milwaukee Avenue; rest rooms available at some shops on the way; no public rest rooms

The Logan Square ride is a study in Chicago boulevards. There are few other places in Chicago that feature so many boulevards this close to one another. As you drive to Humboldt Park, you'll pass beneath the first of two Puerto Rican Flag sculptures that arch over Division Street. At the second one, you'll find the beginning of the ride.

Though there are facilities in Humboldt Park, there are few elsewhere along the ride. Plan on filling your water bottle here and waiting until later to grab a bite.

Named for a German scientist made famous by his notion of living within nature and not against it, Humboldt is big for a city park. There's actually a beach within it, manned by a lifeguard in the summer. Two big lagoons are at its center. As you ride through, you'll notice an inexplicable Leif Eriksson statue erected at some point with neighborhood funding. Even if Vikings were here once, it's a mostly Hispanic neighborhood these days (and a proud one at that).

After you bike through Humboldt Park, you'll find Humboldt

DIRECTIONS
FOR
THE RIDE

0.0 Start at southern end of Humboldt Park.
0.2 Turn right onto Humboldt Boulevard.
2.1 Turn right onto Logan Boulevard.
2.6 Turn left onto Campbell Avenue.
2.7 Turn left onto northern part of Logan Boulevard.
3.4 Ride around Logan Square.
3.6 Turn left onto Kedzie Avenue.
5.5 Reenter Humboldt Park.
5.7 Return to parking lot.

Boulevard at the center of its northern edge. This is a large byway with two-way traffic in the center and less frequented side streets separated by grassy tree-lined patches. As you ride up on the eastern side, you'll pass a sign pointing out a previous home of the famous Frank Baum, writer of *The Wonderful Wizard of Oz*.

As you continue northward your surroundings will grow a bit more run down until you reaching Logan Boulevard. Once again, streets on the outskirts are easy to bike down. The homes on both sides of the street are old and charming, many built in the Prairie Style of architecture. These boulevards were constructed as a result of a Chicago real-estate boom in the late nineteenth century. You'll bike up one way and down the other then arrive at Logan Square—which is in fact a rotary.

Take the rotary three-quarters of the way around and turn down Kedzie, yet another boulevard with two grassy areas in the middle. You'll see even larger flats down this quiet street. You'll eventually come to the northwestern border of Humboldt Park. To finish your day with a sampling of Chicago's Mexican food that many say is among the best in the city, seek out Abril at 2607 North Milwaukee Avenue. By the way, in this part of the city, Milwaukee Avenue is also a boulevard.

Veteran Acres

Number of miles:	7.1
Approximate pedaling time:	2 hours
Terrain:	Hilly
Traffic:	None
Things to see:	Pine forest
Food and facilities:	Food is available in Crystal Lake; rest rooms at park entrance

What's most surprising about Veteran Acres is that it hasn't been totally wrecked by mountain bikers. It's hilly but not rustic, and it's well insulated from the surrounding community. Though this area is by no means far from Chicago, it is very suburban because it's so far north. It's at the northern edge of a community known as Crystal Lake. The lake itself is renowned for hosting a boating event that raises $30,000 every year for local charities—the Corrugated Cardboard Cup Regatta. No joke.

Veteran Acres is a 150-acre park named for returning World War II veterans. As you drive into the preserve, you'll see a sizable pond with open grass areas for picnicking and a huge weeping willow across the way. Over near the park building, though, you'll find access to a wooded trail that descends immediately. As you ride through, for a moment you can peer off to the other side of the forest to see a playing field. As I rode onto the wooded trail, I couldn't believe how many chipmunks I saw. I felt I was in backwoods wilderness.

As I rode the trails here I could have sworn that I was breaking the rules, but I was later assured I wasn't. The sign on the way in gave me the impression that I was on an interpretive nature trail.

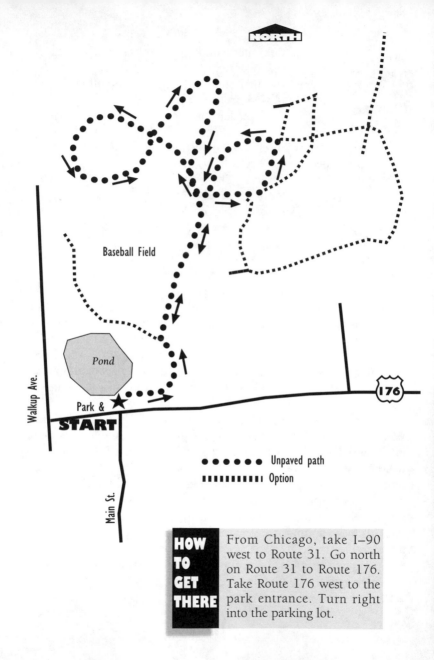

NORTH

Baseball Field

Pond

Walkup Ave.

Park &
START

176

Main St.

● ● ● ● ● Unpaved path
▮▮▮▮▮▮▮ Option

HOW TO GET THERE From Chicago, take I–90 west to Route 31. Go north on Route 31 to Route 176. Take Route 176 west to the park entrance. Turn right into the parking lot.

DIRECTIONS
FOR
THE RIDE

0.0 Enter woods.
0.2 Take right fork.
0.5 Take right fork at prairie opening.
0.8 Take left fork.
2.3 Take left fork.
3.3 Pass straight through intersection.
4.3 Pass straight through intersection.
5.1 Take left fork.
5.3 Take soft fork left.
5.9 Take left fork.
6.2 Take another left fork.
6.6 Take left fork.
7.1 Return to lot.

Because mountain bikers haven't given park managers many problems, they've left trails open.

There are few big hills in the woods as you start out. White paint outlines some of the rocks along the trail—a good ride not to forget your helmet. After a few hills, a final climb brings you out into an open clearing.

There are some enticing options here at the top, but down the hillside of tall prairie grass is a pine forest that looks too good to hold off on. Entering pine forests like these is like entering another world. There's a different hue to everything. Even the temperature seems different: The pine forest seems cooler than the open prairie, but not as cool as the woods. The pine needles do make for less traction; still, smelling pine that doesn't come out of a bottle of air freshener is a bonus of being in the real outdoors.

After twisting through the pines, a few more prairie openings bring you into deep woods in the northwestern portion of the park. Bring a compass and map to find your way through—there are many trail intersections among the loops. While there are next to no facilities out on the trail, the center of town is not far away should you wish for a bite to eat or a drink afterward.

Sag Valley

Number of miles:	12
Approximate pedaling time:	2½ hours
Terrain:	Hilly
Traffic:	None
Things to see:	Toboggan slides, model airplane field
Food and facilities:	Food concessions at Willow Springs Woods; rest rooms on the eastern portion of the trail

Palos is what everybody talks about when they refer to mountain biking in Chicagoland, yet they look at you kind of funny when you mention the Sag Valley. Maybe it's the name. The southern connection of Palos (see ride 25) is Sag Valley, just below the Cal-Sag Channel. The single-track mountain-biking trails at Sag Valley have been retired, but what remains is pretty hilly. It's still a great ride.

You'll start by riding through Paddock Woods, then Palos Park Woods, and on through to Willow Springs Woods. At Willow Springs a massive five-lane toboggan slide is well used by kids of all ages when it reaches 20 degrees outside and there's 4 inches of snow on the ground. Concession stands here also open under about the same conditions. The trail crosses a parking lot on the way to the slide.

Part of Willow Springs Woods has in fact been cleared to preserve the prairie landscape and enhance its growth. Naturally, prairie fires were once a regular part of this landscape. Lightning would strike close to the ground and the whole landscape would burn. This was good because it made the ground more fertile; a greater di-

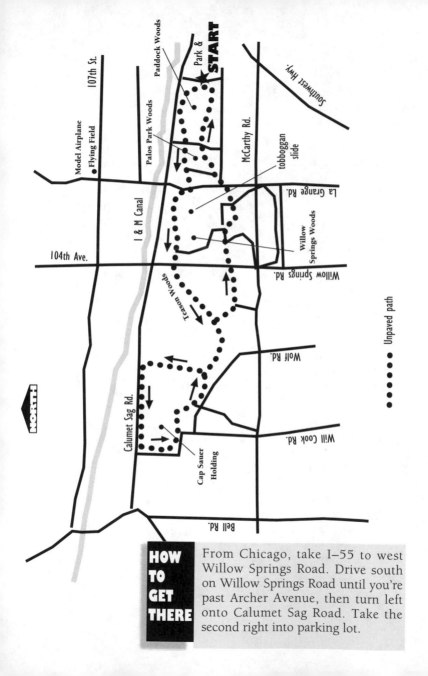

START

Park &

Paddock Woods

107th St.

Model Airplane Flying Field

Palos Park Woods

I & M Canal

104th Ave.

Southwest Hwy.

McCarthy Rd.

La Grange Rd.

tobboggan slide

Willow Springs Woods

Willow Springs Rd.

Teason Woods

Wolf Rd.

Calumet Sag Rd.

Will Cook Rd.

Cap Sauer Holding

Bell Rd.

NORTH

• • • • • • • Unpaved path

HOW TO GET THERE

From Chicago, take I–55 to west Willow Springs Road. Drive south on Willow Springs Road until you're past Archer Avenue, then turn left onto Calumet Sag Road. Take the second right into parking lot.

DIRECTIONS
FOR
THE RIDE

0.0 Turn right onto trail.
0.9 Cross interior road.
1.1 Turn right at fork.
1.5 Cross La Grange Road.
2.3 Turn right at fork.
2.5 Pass Willow Springs Road.
3.5 Turn right at fork.
4.2 Turn right at fork.
7.1 Turn left at fork.
7.5 Turn right at fork.
8.3 Turn right at fork.
8.6 Turn left at fork.
9.2 Pass Willow Springs Road.
9.8 Turn right at second fork.
10.3 Pass La Grange Road and turn left.
10.7 Turn right at fork.
11.0 Pass interior road.
12.0 Return to parking lot.

versity of growth occurs when weeds don't hog the water, killing off weaker plant life. Sag Valley is more wooded than most preserves, but prairies exist here as they do in many Illinois forest preserves.

The eastern portion of the preserve is more parklike, with many picnic areas and parking lots. Once you reach Teason Woods at 104th Street, a well offers water at the top of the hill. After you cross the street, the trail becomes almost entirely wooded. This is a more restricted area; nevertheless, hills abound along the multiuse trails that are open. Fines are levied by trail cops on those found on unauthorized trails. An organization known as the Trail Users Rights Foundation (TURF) sponsors work-and-ride days at which mountain bikers work to replenish eroded and otherwise damaged trails, then ride through the portions still open.

The Cap Sauer Holding in the northwestern portion of Sag Valley is composed of young upland forests and disturbed prairie and oak savanna communities—another prime prairie restoration area. As you ride through, be on the lookout for the red-tailed hawks and turkey vultures that have nested here.

After your ride's complete, head on over to the model airplane flying field at the southwestern corner of La Grange Road and 107th Street. Model airplanes of all shapes and sizes zoom in circles over La Grange Road as remote-controlled-airplane pilots get their kicks.

Des Plaines Trail

Number of miles:	20.4
Approximate pedaling time:	3½ hours
Terrain:	Flat, unpaved
Traffic:	None
Things to see:	Big Bend Lake
Food and facilities:	River Trail Nature Center

Connected to the less developed Indian Boundary Trail (see ride 27), the Des Plaines Trail continues to run along the Des Plaines River. The best place to start is Big Bend Lake. I got there on a rainy fall day and literally watched the leaves fall from the trees as troupes of Canada geese took off and landed. Right near the expressway, it's an easy trail to get to. Though it seems less kept up than other trails, you can't complain about it, because it keeps you in the woods and away from civilization in an area where civilization is everywhere around you. The Old Orchard Mall is no more than 5 miles away, but while you're on the trail, you'd never know it.

In the fall multicolored leaves completely cover the Des Plaines Trail. This makes for a slippery surface on the colorful fence-lined trail that runs through the forest.

North of Euclid Avenue as the trail continues to parallel the Des Plaines River, the River Trail Nature Center comes into view with little warning. This center offers facilities and exhibits about local plant and animal life. An outdoor exhibit runs into the woods with caged birds of prey that were injured in the wilderness. The center also hosts community events related to the outdoors.

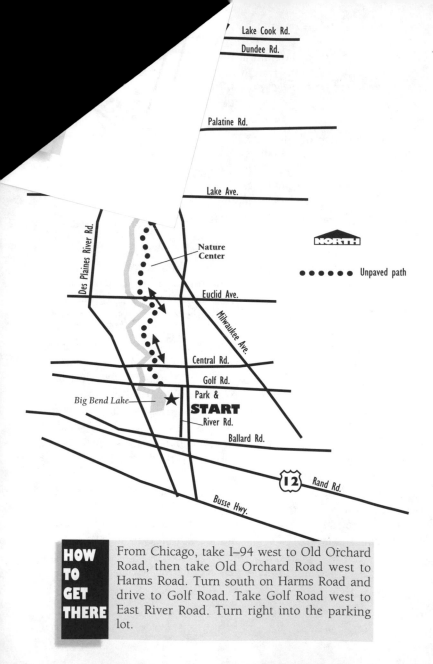

Lake Cook Rd.

Dundee Rd.

Palatine Rd.

Lake Ave.

Des Plaines River Rd.

Nature Center

NORTH

●●●●● Unpaved path

Euclid Ave.

Milwaukee Ave.

Central Rd.

Golf Rd.

Big Bend Lake

Park &
START
River Rd.

Ballard Rd.

12 Rand Rd.

Busse Hwy.

HOW TO GET THERE
From Chicago, take I–94 west to Old Orchard Road, then take Old Orchard Road west to Harms Road. Turn south on Harms Road and drive to Golf Road. Take Golf Road west to East River Road. Turn right into the parking lot.

DIRECTIONS

FOR
THE RIDE

0.0 Start at Big Bend Lake. Turn left onto
      trail from the entrance to the parking lot.
0.3 Cross Golf Road.
2.2 Cross Central Road.
3.7 Cross Euclid Avenue.
5.9 Cross Milwaukee Avenue.
6.2 Cross Palatine Road.
8.0 Cross Dundee Road.
10.2 Turn around at Lake Cook Road.
20.4 Return to parking lot.

The Des Plaines Trail, along with the river that runs along it, is
a sort of twin to the North Branch Trail (see ride 11) with its ad-
joining river, which also runs north and south across Illinois. The
difference is that the area around the Des Plaines River is larger—
close to forty-one hundred acres—more enclosed, and less
crowded.

Bluegills, largemouth bass, and trout can be found in the lakes
and rivers in the Des Plaines Preserve. You'll see a dam south of
Dundee Road. Maples north of Palatine Road drop sizable leaves
along the trail; white trilliums grow past the nature center. Nature
is all around you.

A definite must for a fall ride here is your camera. Instead of
checking out the new fall colors at Old Orchard Mall, come to Des
Plaines at just the right time. These fall colors—the ones you see
outdoors, the ones you knew better back when you were
younger—are richer and more vibrant than any fabric or ink dye
sold at a store.

CHICAGO

ILLINOIS
U.S
66

Historical Route

STARTS
HERE

Route 66 Starting Point

Number of miles:	7.2
Approximate pedaling time:	1½ hours
Terrain:	Flat, paved
Traffic:	Heavy car traffic during the week
Things to see:	Sears Tower, Cook County Hospital
Food and facilities:	Penelope's Cafe, the Original Lou Mitchell's, Sears Tower; no public rest rooms

What's more appropriate to say than "Route 66 Rocks"? The mother road, the main street of America, the glory road, starts in the heart of Chicago at Grant Park. This ride takes you past some downtown Chicago landmarks. It travels busy city streets; best to take this ride on a weekend, when few people frequent this huge grid of office buildings.

Signs strapped to streetlights along Jackson Boulevard indicate the start of Route 66 at Grant Park. In 1977 signs marking the end of Route 66 were taken down from these very posts as an indication that the road's best days were over. It's hard to believe that Route 66 was the first paved road in Illinois; now the city that built itself up around this route pays tribute to it.

As you ride out you'll head west on Jackson then turn right onto Michigan Avenue to avoid going against one-way traffic. On the way west you'll pass 1 block north of a well-known and well-liked German restaurant, Berghoff.

If you continued along this route, it would (slowly) take you to St. Louis and beyond. Once upon a time it was the best way to get all the way to Santa Monica, California—2,400 miles later. This fa-

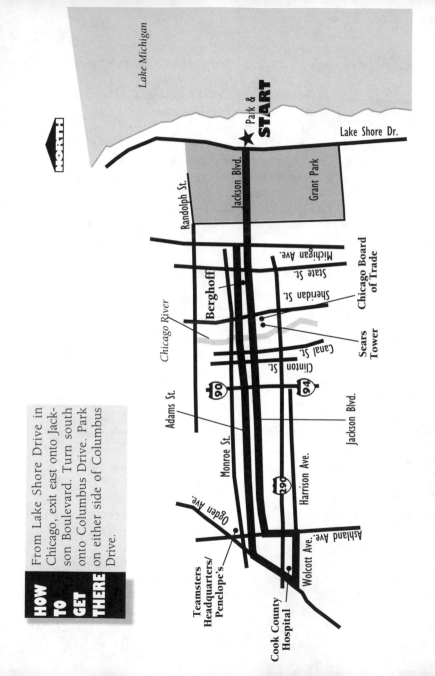

HOW TO GET THERE

From Lake Shore Drive in Chicago, exit east onto Jackson Boulevard. Turn south onto Columbus Drive. Park on either side of Columbus Drive.

NORTH

Lake Michigan

Park & **START**

Lake Shore Dr.

Randolph St.

Jackson Blvd.

Grant Park

Michigan Ave.

State St.

Sheridan St.

Berghoff

Chicago River

Chicago Board of Trade

Canal St.

Clinton St.

Sears Tower

Adams St.

90

94

Jackson Blvd.

Monroe St.

Harrison Ave.

290

Ogden Ave.

Ashland Ave.

Wolcott Ave.

Teamsters Headquarters/ Penelope's

Cook County Hospital

DIRECTIONS
FOR
THE RIDE

0.0 Head west on Jackson Boulevard.
0.3 Turn right onto Michigan Avenue.
0.4 Turn left onto Adams Street.
0.6 Pass Berghoff restaurant.
1.0 Pass Sears Tower on left.
1.2 Cross bridge over Chicago River.
1.5 Cross over expressway.

2.6 Cross Ashland Avenue (Penelope's is between Jackson Boulevard and Adams Street).
3.2 Turn left onto Ogden Avenue.
3.5 Pass Cook County Hospital.
3.6 Turn left onto Wolcott Avenue. Turn left again onto Harrison Street.
3.8 Turn left onto Ashland Avenue.
4.0 Turn right onto Jackson Boulevard.
6.2 Pass Sears Tower.
6.4 Pass Chicago Board of Trade.
7.2 Return to Grant Park.

mous byway is remembered in the words of Kerouac and Steinbeck, through TV and popular song, and—most of all—in the memories of the people who rode it as children.

Once you're over the river and then past the expressway, you'll be heading into a more working-class section of the city. After crossing Ashland Avenue, note the headquarters of the Teamsters a block down. This section of the city is slowly undergoing revitalization as new town houses are being built on nearby streets.

Farther along you'll pass the entrance to the Cook County Hospital, where portions of the movie *The Fugitive* (starring Harrison Ford) were filmed. Much of this area is considered Little Italy; this is most apparent on nearby Taylor Street, with its row of Italian restaurants.

As you make your way back into the city on Jackson Boulevard, you'll pass a famous Route 66 landmark, the Original Lou

Mitchell's, which serves a free cup of sherbet with every meal. A mature waitstaff will serve you anything from pancakes to hamburgers. After you cross the Chicago River, the entrance to the Sears Tower Sky Deck is ahead; soon after, you'll pass the Chicago Board of Trade. Head to the top of the Sears Tower to see all of Chicago or into the Board of Trade to see what the trading floor looks like.

On your way back into the city, notice the brown-and-white signs that run through the Loop and, indeed, the entire state of Illinois, telling that you're on Historic Route 66.

Milwaukee Lakefront

Number of miles:	5.9
Approximate pedaling time:	2 hours
Terrain:	Flat, paved
Traffic:	None
Things to see:	Beachfront, McKinley Marina
Food and facilities:	Concessions and rest rooms at McKinley and Bradford Beaches

Because we live in northwestern Illinois, whenever we Chicagoans head south and west it takes forever to get out of the state. Getting to Milwaukee, however, is always faster than we think. It's possible to make the drive in an hour and a half if you set out early on a weekend. Milwaukee has long been an outlet for Chicagoans who are sick of the familiarity of their urban home. It's not unthinkable to drive to Milwaukee for the day and be back for dinner that night.

We're so used to the idea of riding along Lake Michigan in Chicago that we sometimes forget we share this lake with other cities. Surprisingly, however, we also share some of the same east–west street names, like Green Bay Road and North Avenue. The approach to Milwaukee is much easier than that to Chicago; you don't have to drive through the horrible South Side or dangerous Gary, Indiana. On the way into Milwaukee, you just shoot over a bridge and you're there.

Parking is best and pretty cheap at the Milwaukee Art Museum (MAM) near Veterans Park, although free parking is located farther north. The Milwaukee Lakefront Trail used to be called the Milwaukee 76 Trail to honor the bicentennial, but many of the trails

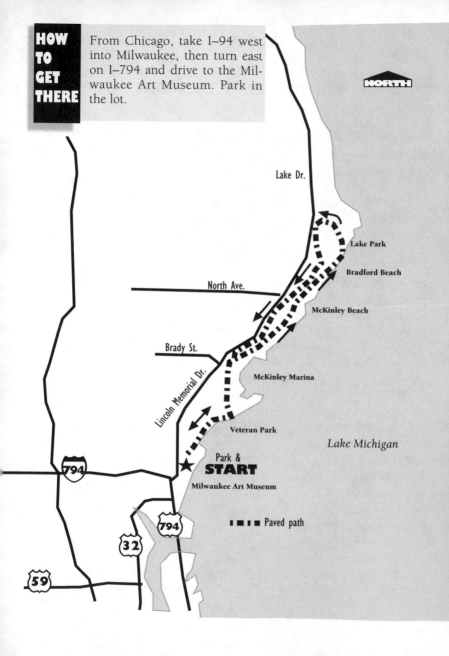

HOW TO GET THERE

From Chicago, take I–94 west into Milwaukee, then turn east on I–794 and drive to the Milwaukee Art Museum. Park in the lot.

NORTH

Lake Dr.

Lake Park

Bradford Beach

North Ave.

McKinley Beach

Brady St.

McKinley Marina

Lincoln Memorial Dr.

Veteran Park

Lake Michigan

794

Park &
START

Milwaukee Art Museum

794

32

59

■ ▮ ■ Paved path

DIRECTIONS
FOR
THE RIDE

0.0 Begin the trail on the lakefront, heading
away from the museum.
0.6 Turn right along interior road.
1.3 Pass McKinley Beach.
2.4 Pass Bradford Beach.
2.8 Turn away from Lake Michigan.
5.9 Return to parking lot.

that run through the city are now called the Oak Leaf Trail. There's this one that runs along the lake; another runs along the river, and still others through some of the city parks.

After you ride past wide-open Veterans Park, which extends from along the shore out to a tip of the shoreline, McKinley Marina comes into view. The Milwaukee lakefront is less crowded than Chicago's, because it's less connected to the city. There are still crowds that you should be aware of, however.

On the other side of the marina, McKinley and Bradford Beaches are well used in the summer. As you ride along the beach, Lake Drive is to your left and Lake Park is ahead.

Over the summer many festivals occur here at the lakefront, just as they do at Chicago's Grant Park. Summerfest is the biggest, but you can also attend Africanfest, Germanfest, Irishfest, and others. It's best to call ahead or check the paper before heading out. In what Milwaukeeans like to call the "Genuine American City," there are many other distractions as well.

Oak Leaf River Trail

Number of miles:	16.6
Approximate pedaling time:	3½ hours
Terrain:	Flat, paved
Traffic:	Moderate
Things to see:	Milwaukee River
Food and facilities:	Picnic tables at Lincoln Park; rest rooms at Lincoln Park and Milwaukee Art Museum

The Oak Leaf River Trail offers you a nice "soft-shelled" way to get to know Milwaukee. As the Milwaukee River makes its way through the northern reaches of the city, a ribbon of park winds with it. Park at the Milwaukee Art Museum (MAM) and ride along the outer stretch of Veterans Park.

The Oak Leaf Trail began quietly in 1939 from a group of bike enthusiasts who were revolutionary in thinking that bike usage could be recreational and not merely functional. By 1964 a newly established Milwaukee County Park Commission took up these efforts by assisting in the design of a loop trail throughout the city. The trail is entirely paved and features many places to stop along the way. Many of the parks are not the type to offer parking lots, but rather the kind you might stroll through or sit down in to read the paper on a bench. Aside from a few places where you'll have to stop on account of traffic, you can pick up some good speed in these parks without causing too much of a stir.

At McKinley Marina the trail departs from the lake to head north through often uncongested city streets. Compared to

Chicago, Milwaukee is a very residential city. The trail remains well marked for most of its way through.

After Estabrook Park, the trail opens up into Lincoln Park as the Milwaukee River widens into a large pond before moving onward. Picnic tables, great trees, and open fields line Lincoln Park. For this ride you'll turn around here at Lincoln, but the trail continues farther—through Riverside Park, Gordon Park, and Kern Park, passing the University of Wisconsin's Milwaukee campus on the right. Trail use increases in these parts due to all the college kids out for a ride or run.

Once you're back at the start, don't forget to stop in at the Milwaukee Art Museum, which prominently backs up to Lake Michigan high above almost anything else. A self-proclaimed "masterpiece on the lakefront," the museum was designed by famed architect Eero Saarinen. Built in 1957 as part of the landmark War Memorial Center, the museum includes a 1975 addition designed by David Kahler. A major expansion designed by Spanish architect Santiago Calatrava is under way and slated to open in 2000. The museum's collection includes more than twenty thousand works of art, from ancient to contemporary; you'll find fifteenth- to twentieth-century European and American paintings, along with sculptures, prints, drawings, photographs, decorative arts, and folk art.

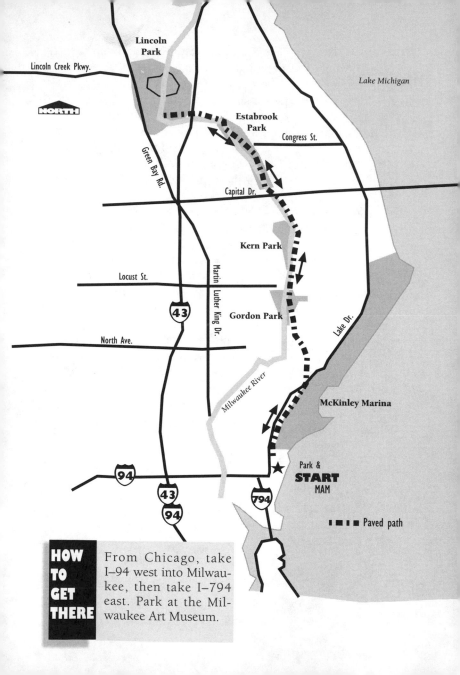

Lincoln Creek Pkwy.

Lincoln Park

Lake Michigan

NORTH

Green Bay Rd.

Estabrook Park

Congress St.

Capital Dr.

Kern Park

Locust St.

Martin Luther King Dr.

Gordon Park

North Ave.

Lake Dr.

Milwaukee River

McKinley Marina

43

94

43
94

794

Park &
START
MAM

★

🟥🟥🟥 Paved path

HOW TO GET THERE

From Chicago, take I–94 west into Milwaukee, then take I–794 east. Park at the Milwaukee Art Museum.

DIRECTIONS

FOR
THE RIDE

0.0 Take main route of Oak Leaf Trail, visible from the parking lot.

2.1 Follow signs leaving lakefront area at McKinley Marina to pick up river at Gordon Park.

4.1 Enter Estabrook Park.

6.3 Turn left after Capital Drive.

7.9 Enter Lincoln Park.

8.3 Turn around at end of Lincoln Park.

16.6 Return to parking lot.

Overview of the Rides

		Historic	Mountain Biking	Rail Trail	In the Country
1	Belmont/Armitage				
2	Southport Ride				
3	Busse Woods				
4	Lakefront North				
5	Lakefront South				
6	Chain O' Lakes			●	
7	Fox River North				
8	Hyde Park	●			
9	Lincoln Park Ride				
10	Deer Grove Preserve		●	●	
11	North Branch Trail				
12	Old Plank Road				●
13	Waterfall Glen		●	●	
14	Bong State Recreation		●	●	●
15	Kettle Moraine South		●	●	●
16	Illinois Prairie Path			●	
17	Salt Creek Trail	●			
18	Great River Trail				
19	I & M Canal State Trail	●		●	
20	Skokie Trail				
21	Robert McClory South			●	
22	Great Western Trail			●	●
23	Fox River South			●	
24	Robert McClory North				
25	Palos		●		
26	Hennepin Canal Feeder			●	●
27	Indian Boundary		●		
28	Rock Island State Trail			●	●
29	Tinley Creek		●		
30	Prairie Avenue Historic				
31	River North	●			
32	Uptown	●			
33	Bohemian Bucktown				
34	Logan Square	●			
35	Veteran Acres		●		
36	Sag Valley		●		
37	Des Plaines Trail				
38	Route 66	●			
39	Milwaukee Lakefront				
40	Oak Leaf River Trail				

Suburbs Through Trees	In the Preserve Proper	Exploring Chicago's Neighborhoods	Cityscape	
		●		**1**
		●		**2**
●				**3**
			●	**4**
			●	**5**
●	●			**6**
				7
		●		**8**
		●		**9**
●	●			**10**
●				**11**
●				**12**
●	●			**13**
	●			**14**
	●			**15**
				16
●	●			**17**
●				**18**
●				**19**
●				**20**
●	●			**21**
				22
				23
●				**24**
●				**25**
●	●			**26**
				27
●	●			**28**
				29
●	●			**30**
			●	**31**
		●		**32**
		●		**33**
		●		**34**
●	●			**35**
	●			**36**
●	●			**37**
	●		●	**38**
			●	**39**
		●		**40**

Appendix

Biking Organizations

Arlington Heights Bicycle Association
500 East Minor Street
Arlington Heights, IL 60004
(847) 657–7105

Chicago Cycling Club
P.O. Box 577136
Chicago, IL 60657-7136
(773) 509–8093

Chicagoland Bicycle Federation
417 South Dearborn Street
Suite 1000
Chicago, IL 60605
(312) 42–PEDAL

Evanston Bicycle Club
P.O. Box 1981
Evanston, IL 60204
(847) 866–7743

Folks on Spokes
P.O. Box 824
Homewood, IL 60430
(708) 730–5179

League of Illinois Bicyclists
417 South Dearborn Street
Suite 1000

Chicago, IL 60605
(708) 481–3429

Mt. Prospect Bike Club
411 South Maple Street
Mt. Prospect, IL 60056-3839
(847) 255–5380

Oak Park Bicycle Club
P.O. Box 2331
Oak Park, IL 60303
(708) 802–BIKE

Recreation for Individuals Dedicated to the Environment (RIDE)
208 South La Salle Street, Suite 1700
Chicago, IL 60604
(312) 853–2820 or (800) 458-2358, ext. 105

Starved Rock Cycling Association
P.O. Box 2304
Ottawa, IL 61350
(815) 434–6673

Trail Users Rights Foundation (TURF)

P.O. Box 403
Summit, IL 60501-0403
(847) 470–4266

Bicycle Clubs

Aurora Bicycle Club
P.O. Box 972
Aurora, IL 60507
(630) 898–5992

Bicycle Club of Lake County
P.O. Box 521
Libertyville, IL 60048
(847) 680–0966

Dundee Bicycle Club
319 North River Street
East Dundee, IL 60118
(847) 622–4100

Elmhurst Bicycle Club
P.O. Box 902
Elmhurst, IL 60126
(630) 415–BIKE

Evanston Bicycle Club
P.O. Box 1981
Evanston, IL 60204-1981
(847) 866–7743

Flyer Bicycle Club
313 S. 11th Avenue
St. Charles, IL 60174

(630) 323–4672

League of Illinois Bicyclists
49 Valley Road
Highland Park, IL 60035

McHenry County Bicycle Club
P.O. Box 917
Crystal Lake, IL 60039
(815) 477–6858

Naperville Bicycle Club
320 West Jackson Avenue
Naperville, IL 60540-5252
(630) 357–9000, ext. 616

Wheeling Wheelmen
P.O. Box 581-D
Wheeling, IL 60097
(847) 520–5010

Chicago Bike Shops

Bike Stop
1034 West Belmont Avenue
(773) 868–6800

Cycle Smithy
2468 North Clark Street
(773) 281–0444

Erehwon Mountain Outfitter
1800 North Clybourn Avenue
(312) 337–6400

Grand Cycle Inc.
7160 West Grand Avenue
(312) 637–0944

Kozy's Cyclery
610 South La Salle Street
(312) 360–0020

Out Spoken
1400 West Belmont Avenue
(312) 404–2919

Performance Bicycle Stop
2720 North Halsted Street
(312) 248–0107

Turin Bicycle
435 East Illinois Street
(312) 923–0100

Urban Bike
4653 North Broadway Street
(773) 728–5212

Village Cycle Center
1337 North Wells Street
(312) 751–2488